THE ENERGY THEORY OF VALUE
AND ITS CONSEQUENCES

TIM WATKINS

Waye Forward (Publishing) Ltd

Llanishen

Cardiff

CF14 5FA

www.publishing.wayeforward.com

ISBN-13: 978-0993087783

ISBN-10: 0993087787

CONTENTS

Tim Watkins graduated from University of Wales College Cardiff with a First Class economic science degree in 1990.

From 1990 to 1997 he worked as a policy researcher with the Welsh Consumer Council where he wrote and published several key policy reports including: *Quality of Life and Quality of Service* – an investigation into the provision of residential care homes for older people - and *In Deep Water* – an investigation into the many problems that followed the North Wales (Towyn) floods of February 1990.

Between 1998 and 2010, Tim Watkins worked for the charity Depression Alliance Cymru, initially as a development worker, and between 2003 and 2010 as its Director. During that time he produced several mental health publications for the charity.

Between 2001 and 2010 Tim Watkins was appointed to sit on several Welsh Government advisory bodies including the Health and Wellbeing Council for Wales, the Burrows-Greenwell Review of Mental Health Services in Wales and the Expert Panel on Depression.

Tim Watkins has authored a range of mental health and wellbeing self-help books and booklets, together with two books about charities and a guide to the digital self-publishing revolution.

Since 2010, Tim Watkins has carried out research into the economic crisis and the linked crises of energy and climate change. In 2015 he published *The Consciousness of Sheep*, an in-depth examination of the way in which our economic, energy and environmental predicament threatens not just our way of life, but our very survival as a species. In 2015, he also published *Austerity - will kill the economy*, a critique of the economic policies adopted in the UK since 2010; and *Britain's Coming Energy Crisis*, a guide to the UK's particular vulnerabilities in a world without cheap oil.

In 2016, Tim Watkins published *The Root of All Evil: the problem of debt-based money*, which builds on the critique of modern finance set out in *The Consciousness of Sheep*.

Tim Watkins is a qualified Life Coach, he also provides coaching, mentoring and support to other writers.

INTRODUCTION

Why does a car cost more than a bicycle? Why does a bottle of Scotch whisky cost more than a bottle of lemonade? Why does a cake cost more than a biscuit? Why does a frying pan cost more than a spatula?

These apparently simple questions lie at the very heart of our understanding of the way the economy works. And I will argue that by arriving at the wrong answer to them for ideological reasons, time and again economists have inflicted misery and deprivation upon the heads of millions of the poorest and least powerful of our fellow citizens.

At a common sense level, the price of any particular good or service is whatever people are prepared to pay for it. After all, if the price of something is so high that nobody wants to buy it, then to all intents and purposes it is worthless. In the same way, if nobody wants a good or service even if the retailer is prepared to give it away, then it too is worthless.

There is of course another side to the problem. I would, for example, be more than happy to pay £100 for a sports car. So too, I suspect, would millions of my fellow consumers. This is an expression of *desire*, since sports cars are desirable items. However, nobody who is in the business of manufacturing sports cars is ever going to sell one for £100 (at today's prices). So even though there is widespread desire for sports cars, there is considerably less *demand*. Demand refers to the number of potential buyers of a good or service at a given price… the price the retailer is prepared to sell it for.

There are all kinds of reasons why prices might fluctuate. A sudden boost in the value of a currency, for example, would allow consumers to purchase imported goods at a lower price. Technological innovation may serve to drive prices down. In a recession, a retailer may opt for a fire-sale in order to sell off goods for whatever price people are prepared to pay. Nevertheless, there must be some underlying determinant of price that allows us to judge the worth of *any* good or service.

We understand that goods do not magically materialise in the shops. They have to be manufactured. To manufacture goods, we need such things as:

o   Mines and quarries to obtain the raw materials

o   Ships and trucks, roads and ports, cranes and hoists to move the raw materials to processing plants

o   More ships and trucks to move processed materials to assembly factories

o   Machinery and tools to assemble the finished product.

At every stage in the process, we need human (and sometimes animal) workers. We also need finance to pay for it all. Perhaps less obviously, we need an education system of some kind to train the workforce in the various skills required by the manufacturing process. We need medical services to ensure that these skilled workers are not lost to disease. We need courts of law and police forces to enforce contract law so that there can be trust throughout the supply chain. The list could go on, but you get the idea.

Importantly, all of these necessary factors in the production process come at a cost. Workers have to be paid. Machinery and tools have to be purchased. Taxes have to be paid to cover the transport infrastructure, education, health and law and order. All of these (and many other) costs have to be factored into the final price of a good or service.

Time and again we have witnessed what happens when the prices that people are prepared to pay for goods fall below the costs involved in their manufacture. In the UK in 2016 we have seen the collapse of the British Home Stores chain with the loss of 11,000 jobs. We have also seen the closure of several steel plants and the threat of wider closures as a result of a steel glut on world markets. The North Sea oil and gas industry has been decimated by a sustained fall in global prices well below the cost of exploration and recovery.

When closures of this kind occur, we tend to look for someone to blame. This is much easier in cases like British Home Stores, where maverick bosses obviously raped the company – and its pension fund – for personal gain; using tax avoidance schemes to prevent the state recovering at least some of the cost of the pensions that taxpayers will now have to take some responsibility for. Extreme cases like this, however, point to a more contentious "cost" within the price of any good or service – *profit*.

Somehow, in the process of creating and exchanging a good or service, its owner(s) will walk away with something more than they put into the process to begin with. Indeed, it is unlikely that anyone would invest in the production of goods and services if there was not a reasonable degree of certainty that they were going to come away with more than they put in. At a break even, they would be as well off leaving their money under the mattress (or, God forbid, in a bank).

The various ways in which economists have sought to explain how price operates has, in large part been concerned with explaining where – and by what mechanism – this something for nothing, profit or "surplus value" comes from. And it is this area of economics that is inevitably ideological and political; because if the profit that accrues to the owners is arrived at fraudulently, then clearly there will be a political conflict between those owners and those from whose share the profit was removed.

At each turn in the development of economics from the French Physiocrats through to the astrologers and alchemists in today's neoclassical school, economists have denied that their theories are in any way tainted by ideology or political motivation. Nevertheless, and not by accident, each of the theories that they arrived at just happened to coincide with the interests of the ruling elites of their day. The Physiocrats, with their claim that profit was ultimately derived from the food we eat, just happened to find themselves aligned with the interests of the landed French aristocracy. The British Classical economists with their belief that profit came from combining capital and labour, mysteriously found themselves on the same side of the argument as Britain's emerging capitalist class of factory and mill owners. Today's Neoclassicals, with their focus on finance and investment as the source of profit simply arrived on the same side of the argument as the modern banking elite by accident.

One school of political economy grew up with a coherent critique of economists and the exploitative systems of production that their ideas serve(d) to support. This was the school of economics developed from the works of the German philosopher Karl Marx.

Where the other economic schools sought to bolster the prevailing economic arrangements, Marx was determined to overthrow them:

"Philosophers seek to understand the world. Our task, however, is to change it."

Marx constructed a theory – developed from the Labour Theory of Value of British classical economists like Adam Smith and David Ricardo – in which profit or surplus value was created by the working class (proletariat) and then expropriated by the capitalist class (bourgeoisie) through a process of exploitation. Unlike most other economic and political philosophers, Marx argued that there was no way by which the interests of capital and labour could be reconciled within the existing system. Therefore, only a revolution could remove the parasitic capitalist class, whose presence had become a fetter on further human development.

While in his later life, Marx rowed back on his early formulation of the Labour Theory of Value – and was moved to say that "I am not a Marxist" – his many followers continue to this day to insist upon the truth of the Labour Theory of Value, and the ever more urgent need for a revolution to overthrow the capitalist system so that humanity can move on to the communist utopia.

Politically, of course, these ideas cast a long shadow across the twentieth century; serving to destabilise Europe in the wake of the First World War and to generate the Cold War between the USA and the USSR (and their respective allies) in the aftermath of the Second World War. In economics – although relegated to the sidelines prior to 2008 – Marx's ideas have seemed sufficiently plausible to enough people to provide a corrective critique to mainstream economics. Since the Great Financial Accident of 2008, a new generation of economics students and graduates have turned to Marx for an explanation of why nothing that they had studied in the course of their economics degree courses had even hinted at an explanation of the global economic turmoil that we now find ourselves in.

This, I believe, puts us in an extremely dangerous position. This is because Marx's Labour Theory of Value is 90 percent correct. And in the volatile political and economic climate of the post-crash global economy, we are once again being pulled in the direction of political extremism. For the most part, this is manifesting in a form of right-wing populism in the shape of Brexit, Donald Trump, Beppe Grillo, UKIP, the Front Nationale and Golden Dawn. However, the unexpected mass appeal of Britain's Jeremy Corbyn and America's Bernie Sanders hints at a population equally prepared to look to socialism for answers. And when both right-wing populism and left-wing social democracy fail to solve the contradictions inherent in the current global economic arrangements, there is a very real risk of the growth of both fascist and communist movements similar to those that emerged in the 1930s.

I believe, however, that an understanding of the 10 percent of the Labour Theory of Value that Marx got wrong (and was stumbling toward at the end of his life) can provide us with a different route map for our collective future; one that will allow us to reconcile most of our differences without the need for the kind of violence seen in the 1930s. It is this alternative route map that I wish to sketch out in this book.

PART I: THE ENERGY THEORY OF VALUE

THE RELATIONSHIP OF VALUE TO WEALTH

In the modern world we tend to think that wealth and money are the same thing. Someone who wins the Lottery, for example, is believed to be wealthy. But money is not so much wealth, but rather a claim on future wealth. That is, if we took the millions of pounds that someone had won on the Lottery, and withdrew them in the form of a pile of £50 notes; it would not be the notes themselves that were worth anything, but rather the goods and services that those notes could purchase. A house, a car, a chicken and an apple are all forms of wealth, but money is not.

Money is supposed to act as a store of wealth. As such, it allows us all to trade with greater ease than might otherwise be the case. For example, I might decide to sell my car and buy a bicycle instead. But it is highly unlikely that the bicycle shop will be prepared to do a straight swap. Moreover, my car might be worth a lot more than the bicycle I want to purchase. Money allows me to convert my existing wealth (my car) into a claim on future wealth (my bicycle together with some additional items that I will purchase with the remainder of the money). When we go to work, we engage in a similar process. The wealth that we sell is our time and skills. At the end of the week or the month, our employer pays us the money equivalent of the time/skills we provided. We then use this money to pay for the various goods and services that we each consume every month.

There is, however, a difference between selling a car and selling our time. When I sold my car, I did not have to wait for a month to get paid. Indeed, I doubt that any of us would be prepared to allow someone to drive off in the car solely on the promise that they will pay for it in a month's time.

When we go to work, we accept this arrangement. And in the event of our employer having cash flow problems or going bust, we risk not getting paid at all.

Fundamentally our employment is debt based. So too is a great deal of the productive process. Investors lend money to a business to help it get an enterprise off the ground. The business owners effectively borrow the capital, labour and resources needed against the promise that they will pay the lenders back – with interest – at some later date. That is, somehow they will generate more wealth at the end of the process than was put in to begin with.

Where does this additional wealth come from? This is where value comes in. The idea is that somewhere in the process of creating goods and services, value is added to make the wealth at the end greater than the wealth at the start. When the end goods and services are sold, they cost more money than is needed to pay back the investors, the workers and the suppliers, and to provide a healthy income for the business owners.

Is this some kind of magic that defies the laws of the universe? I begin with some timber, some screws and some glue. I combine them with some machines, tools and some skilled craftsmen, and I end up with a dining table and chairs. The second law of thermodynamics[1] (the law of entropy)

---

[1] "The Second Law of Thermodynamics is about the *quality* of energy. It states that as energy is transferred or transformed, more and more of it is wasted. The Second Law also states that there is a natural tendency of any isolated system to degenerate into a more disordered state." http://www.livescience.com/50941-second-law-thermodynamics.html

would suggest that the opposite should be true – as, indeed, it would be if I left the table and chairs outside in all weathers for long enough. But somehow, we have managed to take a high entropy (low order) pile of materials and convert them into a low entropy (high order) structure. This is almost as good as discovering the holy grail of perpetual motion.

Alas, there is a far simpler explanation that is entirely consistent with the laws of the universe. Put simply, at least one of the inputs to the production of wealth was not paid its full value. That is, we paid a cheap price for something of far higher value.

Whatever this input was, it would somehow have to evade the general supply and demand market mechanism through which prices are determined. This tends to rule out most of the capital invested in an enterprise because – with the exception of specialist machinery and tools – capital will be bought on the open market. Try to buy a lathe or a hammer on the cheap, and the retailer will simply sell it to someone else. Similarly, the resources required for the enterprise will also be traded on the open market. So again, it is all but impossible to pay less than the resources are worth.

This leads us to one blindingly obvious – and entirely wrong – conclusion: it must be the workers who are paid less than they are worth.

THE LABOUR THEORY OF VALUE

Classical economists like Adam Smith and David Ricardo put forward a Labour Theory of Value in which workers created the added value in the process of production. They were uncomfortable about the implications, however. If the workers were paid less than their value, then by definition, the investors and the business owners were being paid more than they were worth. As such, the entire production process would amount to little more than organised theft; different to slavery only in the methods used to coerce workers into parting with what was rightfully theirs.

Karl Marx had no such discomfort. Having viewed the impoverishment of working people in the industrial cities of England, Marx was convinced that capitalism was indeed organised theft. Moreover, Marx believed that once the workers understood the process through which they were being mugged, they would rise up and overthrow their oppressors. For Marx, the next step was obvious – he had to explain, in writing for all to see, how the process of theft occurred.

The result was Marx's Labour Theory of Value.

Marx argued that there are two components to the value of all goods and services. First, they have a *use* value (since nobody wants to pay for something that is use*less*). Second, they have an *exchange* value. Understanding how this exchange value is arrived at is key to understanding Marx's theory.

Marx reasoned that there must be something common to all goods and services that provided the basis for their price. Whatever this was, it was also the basis of exchange value.

Arguably there are lots of similarities, but there is only one obvious component that every good and service has in common: they contain expended labour. Something as simple as an apple or as complex as a steam locomotive can only exist as a product of labour. Yes, they have capital and resource inputs, but these are seldom the same for every product. Labour by contrast is ubiquitous.

So labour is the source of value. But this does not explain very much. Nobody is claiming that an apple and a steam engine are worth the same. Clearly it takes a lot more labour to produce a locomotive than an apple – and as any novice gardener will tell you from bitter experience, even producing something as simple as an apple takes a degree of skill.

In examining the "more" labour that goes into the steam engine, it is clear that we are talking about time, since this is how labour is deployed. The number of hours required to produce the locomotive is a lot more than is required to grow and pick the apple. But there is a problem with this. If the amount of time required to produce something was what determined its value, then we would do well to invest in the laziest and least competent workers we could find. Clearly these would take much longer to finish the job, and so the end product would be worth much more!

Obviously this was not a description of the world Marx was looking at. Skill, too, came into the equation. Businesses had to employ workers with the requisite skills to produce the goods. Simply hiring incompetents would not generate additional value. Indeed, it was more likely to result in bankruptcy. However, this did not get away from the problem of lazy workers producing more value.

To get past this problem, Marx argued that it was not the time taken by any particular worker that mattered. It was labour in general that provided the measure of value. Across the economy as a whole and given the appropriate capital investment, there would be an average amount of skilled labour time required to produce any given goods or services. Marx referred to this as *socially necessary* labour time. In any economy, there would be some workers and some firms that took longer to produce something (these would lose out) and some who took less time (these would gain) and collectively these would determine the average, and thus the value of labour. This in turn would determine the exchange value.

In normal conditions, the exchange value is similar to a break-even point. It sets the price below which it is no longer worthwhile to produce a good or service. Use value, on the other hand, can vary according to market conditions, and thus affects supply and demand pricing. A good or service might be useful, but *exactly how* useful? For example, the food that you buy has a very strong use value, whereas a magazine or a glass of beer has a weaker use value – you can give it a miss if you are short of cash or have other things you want to buy.

This explained the relationship between labour and value. It did not, however, explain the mechanism whereby capitalists stole the surplus value from the workers. To understand this part of the story, you need to understand what has been termed "the money trick".

THE MONEY TRICK

Remember that you and I are paid wages or a salary in arrears. That is, we work for a week or a month, and we get paid at the end. A few – the elite – make an income entirely from investments. Some business owners enjoy a hybrid arrangement in which they are paid a combined salary (for their work) and dividend (for their investment). Self-employed people are in a slightly worse position to employed workers insofar as they effectively draw wages from a plethora of different employers that they must continuously replace. But the overwhelming majority of the population sell their time and skills to a single employer in exchange for a wage/salary.

This way of doing business has been around for so long that it is taken for granted. However, it was not always that way. Indeed, arguably, since wage labour only emerged as part of the industrial revolution, it is not even the most common way of doing business. In feudal times, people did not work for money at all. Rather, they worked a plot of land granted to them by a landlord. In return, they were obliged to give some of their time to the landlord. They were also obliged to give time to the church, and could expect to have to give up some of their produce in exchange for craft skills; for example, paying the miller for grinding their grain.

As a result of labour shortages in the wake of the fourteenth century Black Death, feudal relationships began to breakdown in favour of cash payments. And as trade progressed, mercantilism emerged as a preferred means of doing business. In this "putting out" system, a merchant would loan (for a fee) a craftsman the tools (capital) required to produce goods. The merchant would also supply the raw materials needed. The merchant would then pay the craftsman for the finished produce. This arrangement was far from free of exploitation. The merchant could easily increase the rental cost for the craftsman's tools, or the price for the raw materials. Alternatively, the merchant could simply lower the price paid for the end produce. Either way, the craftsman lost out. Importantly though, the craftsman could easily see where the money was going. If a merchant became too exploitative, the craftsman could go to work for a different merchant. Alternatively, craftsmen could combine and agree not to work for too low a price. So there were limits on how exploitative merchants could be.

The factory system of the early industrial revolution changed everything. Whereas the mercantilist craftsmen participated in the entire production process, factory workers participated in just a single fraction. Adam Smith famously used the example of pin production to highlight the difference. A craftsman would start with the raw metal. He would use his tools and skills to draw the metal out; cut it to the correct length; sharpen the point; and fasten the head. At the end he would be paid a set amount per pin. In the factory system, by contrast, each worker would have just one part to play. One worker would draw out the metal; another would cut it to length; another would sharpen the point; yet another would fasten the head. But – crucially – none would be paid according to the number of pins produced. Rather, each would receive a payment for the amount of time he or she put in.

So the mechanism by which capitalists stole value from workers was through the trick of hiding their true value and paying them only what was required for them to maintain themselves. That is, just enough to cover their rent, fuel, food and transport. The remainder of the value that workers' labour power created was expropriated (i.e. stolen) by the capitalist and paid out to investors in the form of profit.

Importantly, this theory of how capitalism operates also explains the periodic cycles of crises that are an integral part of any capitalist economy. Marx referred to these as crises of *over-production*; although they are more easily understood as crises of *under-consumption*.

Insofar as capitalists as a whole steal profit from workers as a whole, by paying workers less than the value of the goods and services they produce, then collectively the workers – as consumers – have never got sufficient money to purchase all of the goods and services on sale. But because the economy is complex, and can be temporarily maintained through borrowing and government money printing, the system can be maintained for several years between cyclical recessions. Nevertheless, ultimately workers – as consumers – simply lack the spending power to purchase everything that has been produced. So eventually the least efficient firms go bust, workers are made redundant and the price of goods and labour falls. Eventually prices fall to a point where new investment becomes attractive once again. New jobs are created, workers are able to spend more, prices increase and investment becomes even more attractive. And so the cycle begins once again.

This Marxist Labour Theory of Value appears to be far better aligned to what happens in the real world than any of the theories put forward by the classical or modern neoclassical economists. Indeed, following the spectacular failure of neoclassical economists to either spot or adequately explain the crash of 2008, economics students have been turning to Marx for a possible explanation of what has gone wrong.

On the political front, too, the impact of the crisis on ordinary people's living standards – together with ever more overt corruption on the part of the global elite – has pushed many people toward Marxist and socialistic political parties and movements as an alternative to the failed liberal/social democratic politics of the boom years.

In his later years, however, Marx was moved to proclaim that "I am not a Marxist!" One reason for this is that he had begun to doubt the validity of his own Labour Theory of Value which lay at the very heart of Marxist politics. The problem for Marx lay in the start of a process all too familiar in the modern world – *automation*. As the use of machinery developed during Marx's lifetime, the relationship between workers and machines began to reverse. Whereas in the early industrial revolution machines had most often been an extension of the worker and his tools, as the nineteenth century progressed, workers began to be relegated to the role of machine minders – no longer actively deploying the machinery, but merely standing by in case the machine stopped working.

The problem was that if machines could produce goods without the need for workers (in the way that modern assembly plants do) according to the Labour Theory of Value these goods would have no exchange value because they would contain no labour.

Marx died before completing his epic *Das Kapital* – he completed the first volume, and his compatriot Frederick Engels completed a further two volumes from Marx's notes. The *Grundrisse*[2], which was a kind of outline draft of *Das Kapital*, suggests that Marx intended at least 10 volumes. It may well be that Marx would have reformulated the Labour Theory of Value to account for the increasing automation of production in these unfinished works. Unfortunately, his demise intervened, and it was left to others to pick up where he left off.

By the time Marx died, his Labour Theory of Value had become the basis for communist and socialist movements and parties across Europe and the USA. So long as these groups stuck to the view that labour was the true source of surplus value (i.e. profit), then they could make a convincing case for revolution to overthrow the parasitic capitalist class and return to the workers the full fruits of their labour.

In the real world, however, far from witnessing the transition toward the communist utopia in the developed economies (Marx believed Germany would lead the way) communist revolutions have tended to emerge out of the most backward agrarian societies. This, together with the failure of these regimes to produce an attractive alternative to capitalism, would suggest that there is something amiss with the theory. Not that you would discover what was wrong from modern

[2] *The Grundrisse der Kritik der Politischen Ökonomie* (Outlines of the Critique of Political Economy)

economics; which dismiss or ignore value altogether. For neoclassical economics, all that is required is an understanding of the myriad supply and demand measures of all of the transactions that occur between firms and households. Most economics textbooks present some version of the diagram below as a model of how the economy operates (all else being treated as "externalities"):

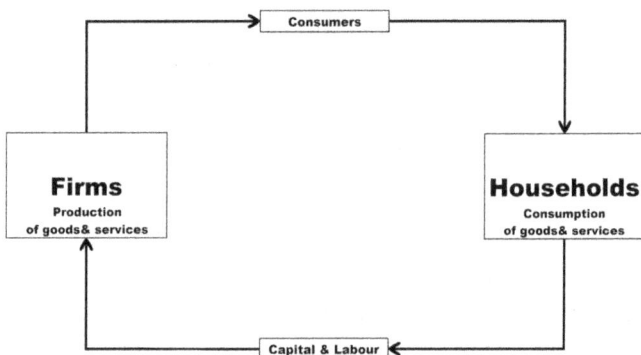

Systems ecologist professor Charles A. Hall has said of this model that were it to be presented by a freshman student, he would grade it A+ for imagination and F- for grounding in science. Indeed, the failure of contemporary economists to either foresee or mitigate the Great Financial Accident of 2008 has led an increasing number of scientists to intervene in economic debates that are all too often more akin to astrology than to genuine science.

Where does this leave us in relation to value? We have a Marxian view of value as labour power versus a neoclassic view that either value doesn't exist or that it plays an insignificant part in the operation of the economy. I beg to differ. I believe that Marx was *almost* correct insofar as he understood that to generate surplus value (profit) at least one of the inputs to the economy must be paid far less than the value that it generates. It is simply that the input in question is not (or at least not primarily) labour.

VALUE AS WORK

Marx would have been the first to accept that philosophers and economists are very much a product of the times and conditions that they live in. He said as much:[3]

> "The ideas of the ruling class are in every epoch the ruling ideas, i.e. the class which is the ruling material force of society, is at the same time its ruling intellectual force. The class which has the means of material production at its disposal, has control at the same time over the means of mental production, so that thereby, generally speaking, the ideas of those who lack the means of mental production are subject to it. The ruling ideas are nothing more than the ideal expression of the dominant material relationships, the dominant material relationships grasped as ideas."

As we have seen, Marx developed his Labour Theory of Value from classical economists of the early industrial revolution; like Adam Smith and David Ricardo. But these economists were merely reformulating the ruling ideas of an ascendant capitalist elite (bourgeoisie) that drew its wealth from the capitalist forms of production. In the same way, an earlier group of economists – the French Physiocrats – had developed their ideas from the dominant form of production in their day; a landed aristocracy that was destined to be replaced by industrial capitalism.

The Physiocrats believed that value came from the land, and the food that it produced. Quite correctly, they noted that without food there could be no workers, no labour power and ultimately no capital. The factory system might serve

[3] From *The German Ideology.* 1845.

to obscure this core fact, but did not negate it. Even in today's complex global economy it would be difficult (though not impossible[4]) to argue that we could have a functioning economy without food.

At a time when more than two-thirds of the population were directly engaged in agriculture, it was fairly easy to make the argument that food was the source of value. Today, with less than one percent of us (in the developed countries) engaged in agriculture, it is much harder. In the same way, it was far easier to argue that labour was the source of value when a rapidly growing proportion of the population was engaged in the production of goods and services. It might be that both propositions were wrong. There is, however, an alternative proposition that incorporates and unifies both positions into a greater whole.

Both Marx and the Physiocrats were largely correct. However, neither stepped back sufficiently to fully understand the basic nature of value. Each, constrained by the level of understanding in their respective systems of production, missed something even more fundamental as a source of all value. Crucially, as in Marx's Labour Theory of Value, this "something more fundamental" would have to generate significantly more value than it actually cost to input into the system of production.

Even in the Physiocrats' time, automation existed in a rudimentary form. For while it is true that almost all work involved labour power, there were important exceptions.

[4] Artificial Intelligence theorists are currently concerned about the potential threat from intelligent machines that, in theory, could continue to exist even if humanity went extinct.

Millers used water wheels and windmills to power the giant mill stones that ground grain. Blacksmiths used charcoal (and later coal) in the production of steel weapons and tools. Even agricultural workers used plough horses and oxen in the production of food. For hundreds of years, trade had depended upon wind powered sailing ships to move goods across the world's seas and oceans.

So neither workers nor the food they ate were the source of value. Those economists who said that they were had simply failed to follow their own logic back far enough. The one key component that labour brings to production is human creativity. Someone has to design the axe, the boat, the steam engine or the motor car *before* it can be built. But at the points in history when Marx or the Physicrats were writing, most of what most workers brought to production was plain simple energy – the effort required to swing the sledgehammer or dig the earth.

The average human can generate 155 Kilowatt hours of energy in a working year. In the eighteenth century, this would have been pushed slightly higher by obliging people to work longer hours. Since, along with working animals, this would have been the only energy input to the productive process, Marx was entirely correct to argue that profit resulted from not paying enough for the energy input. However, in their own way, the Physiocrats were also correct to argue that since that energy ultimately came from the food that the workers (and work animals) consumed, then without agriculture, the economy could not exist.

This is thermodynamics in action. And unlike economic and political laws (such as the speed limit on a modern road), the laws of thermodynamics cannot be broken. What the first law of thermodynamics tells us is that you can neither create nor destroy energy; you can merely transform it. Calories in the food that we eat are converted into kinetic energy by human (and animal) muscles. We (and animals) also produce unusable heat when we work our muscles. This is the second law of thermodynamics in action. The second law says that in any conversion of energy from one state to another, some energy is always lost (as heat) and cannot be used. Using food to power workers to operate an economy tends to be inefficient.

This said, the process through which plants obtain energy is also inefficient. Most of the sunlight that plants use in the process of photosynthesis goes to waste. Only through the ongoing development of human agriculture have we developed strains of plants that store relatively large amounts of energy in the form of sugars and starches to provide us with the calories we need (and in the West, far more than we need) to operate the economy.

Notice that neither plants nor sunlight feature in the models of the economy used by modern economists. Either they are assumed to be on hand whenever they are required or they are deemed to be unimportant. This flies in the face of, for example, the February 1917 Russian Revolution and the 2011 Arab Spring which, at least in part, were the result of food shortages. Indeed, almost all of the bloody revolutions in human history began as food riots.

Contrarian economist professor Steve Keen has observed that:

"Labour without energy is a corpse and capital without energy is a statue."

To be in any way an accurate model of the real world, any economic model would have to begin with the sunlight with which plants produce the calories that keep people alive. Professor Hall argues that at the very least, a model would have to involve four components:

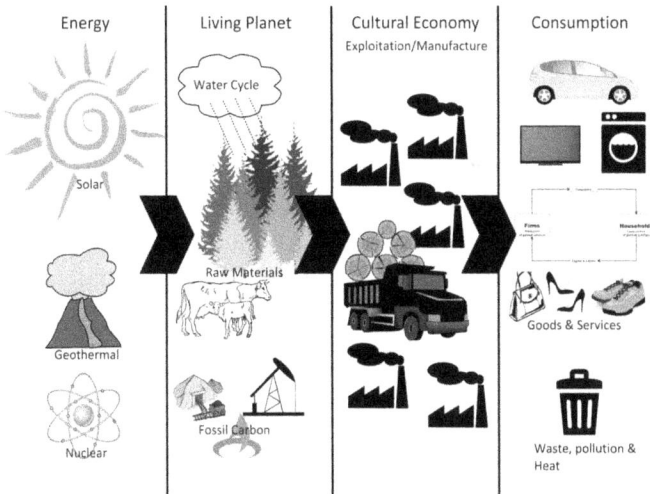

Beginning with energy, which comes primarily from the sun but also includes some geothermal and nuclear, we have to have the processes that interact to allow life on Earth. We also have to include geothermal processes that produce mineral deposits. Without these inputs, we can have no cultural (i.e. human) economy. What humanity does is first, to exploit raw materials – for example, turning trees into lumber – and second, to fashion these exploited raw materials into manufactured goods. Only when all of this – which accounts for the bulk of the energy and resources required – has been done can we have the economic circulation between firms and households that economists think is all that the economy consists of.

In the diagram I have placed waste, pollution and heat at the end of the process for illustrative purposes; not least because consumption in the developed countries is unconscionably wasteful.[5] In reality, waste, pollution and heat are a by-product at every stage in the process, and are the manifestation of the second law of thermodynamics.

One reason why Marx may have missed the importance of solar energy and the interaction of sunlight with the living Earth is that nobody was sure at that time where fossil carbons such as coal and oil came from. By the early 1930s, Noble Prize winning chemist and economist Frederick Soddy understood that coal (and oil and gas) were, in effect, millions of years of fossilised sunlight:[6]

"Still one point seemed lacking to account for the phenomenal outburst of activity that followed in the Western world the invention of the steam engine, for it could not be ascribed simply to the substitution of inanimate energy for animal labour… The profound

[5] This is usually unseen because the pollution and heat is generated in developing countries where the goods consumed in the West were manufactured.

[6] Soddy, F. 1933. *Wealth and Debt: The solution of the economic paradox.* Britons Publishing Company.

change that then occurred seemed to be rather due to the fact that, for the first time in history, men began to tap a large *capital* store of energy and ceased to be entirely dependent on the *revenue* of sunshine.

"With the doctrine of evolution, the real Adam turns out to have been an animal, and with the doctrine of energy the real capitalist proves to be a plant. The flamboyant era through which we have been passing is due not to our own merits, but to our having inherited accumulations of solar energy from the carboniferous era, so that life for once has been able to live beyond its income. Had it but known it, it might have been a merrier age!"

At the start of the Industrial Revolution, Britain contained as much energy in the form of coal as Saudi Arabia contained in the form of oil. So abundant was this fossilised solar energy, that – to begin with at least – it could simply be picked up from the ground or hacked from exposed seems on the side of hills. Later, the development of the steam engine allowed deep mining, and formed the basis of the factories, railways and steam ships that revolutionised manufacture and trade in the nineteenth century. But because it is solid, coal is an awkward energy source. It can be converted to liquid, but only at high cost. As a solid, there are limits to its use and mobility.

By the end of the nineteenth century another, far more versatile fossil carbon was coming into production. The first oil production in Pennsylvania and Oklahoma was in response to a rapid decline in the whale population. People had used whale oil for lighting, but they now turned to kerosene as a cheaper and cleaner alternative. This provided the springboard for the US oil industry to take off. However, it was two waste products of the kerosene industry that were to shape the world as we know it; a liquid called diesel oil, and a gas called petrol or gasoline.

In the developed countries there is almost nothing that we consume that was not transported in a diesel-powered lorry. Indeed, if we add together all of the raw materials that are used in the manufacture of all of the goods that we consume (including the goods required to deliver a service), we often find that in addition to several lorry journeys, there will have also been diesel-powered machinery involved in extraction, and diesel-powered shipping involved in transportation. In addition, much of the manufacturing process will have been powered by electricity generated from coal.

When we begin to see how much work we derive from fossil fuels, we start to understand what Marx and the Physocrats missed given the relative underdevelopment of their day. Imagine for a moment that your car broke down seven miles from home. Imagine that you had no choice but to push it home on your own. How long might that take you? It would probably take a fortnight or even a month of backbreaking labour to get home. And yet for about £1.10 you can buy a litre of petrol or diesel that will allow you to get your car home in about seven minutes. This is an illustration of just how much work – or *value* – fossil fuels provide.

Even today we have a cultural blind spot to the massive amount of work that energy-dense fossil carbon fuels have provided us with for the best part of three centuries. Consider our current consumption of three fossil carbons – gas, coal and oil. In the UK, on average per year we each use 4,633,000 cubic feet of gas; 1,473 tons of coal; and 8.76 barrels of oil (this, of course, excludes the fossil carbon already embodied in the goods and services that we import). We only consume a fraction of this fossil carbon directly to heat our homes or to drive our cars. Most of it is used to power our businesses, generate our electricity and to transport our goods and services.

While we normally focus on the price of energy, if we convert our consumption into kilowatt hours (KW/h) we can begin to get an idea of the value they give us. Taken together, we each on average use 20,998KW/h of energy per year from the gas, coal and oil that our economy consumes. Contrast this with the paltry 155KW/h that the average human labourer can provide each year. In effect, fossil fuels provide us with 136 years of labour power for every person in the UK – roughly 8.7 billion years' worth of work!

Paid at the 2014 average wage of £26,000 this would provide each of us with an additional £3,600,615 worth of work every year – a staggering £230,799,466,000,000 worth of hidden, uncomplaining and largely unpaid labour without which our civilisation would simply collapse.

Remember too that these calculations apply solely to the fossil fuels burned directly within the UK. A large part of the goods that we consume were produced in someone else's country; most notably China, which has emerged as the second highest energy consuming country on the planet. If this energy were added to the energy we burn directly, we could more than double the £230 trillions' worth of work that we enjoy the benefits of at next to no cost.

Marx's basic proposition was that to produce surplus value/profit at the end of the process of production and exchange, some input has to be providing more than it cost. Marx was also correct to identify this input as *work*. Where Marx went wrong – more understandable then than now – was to conflate work with human labour. Because while human labour is indeed work; work is not solely or even mostly the product of labour. For the best part of three centuries we have been able to obtain extremely low-cost fossil carbon. It is the hyper-exploitation of this resource – not human labour power – that explains the massive expansion of production and consumption that began in the eighteenth century with the Industrial Revolution.

The working class were not robbed of what was rightfully theirs via the production process (other than in the sense that humanity as a whole could have made far more effective and rational use of the Earth's limited fossil carbon deposits). There are other means by which both capital and labour are stolen from via the debt-based monetary system at the heart of modern financial capitalism. However, in terms of the source of surplus value, the real "exploitation" was of the billions of uncomplaining "fossil fuel slaves" on the back of which the modern world was built.

THE TENDENCY FOR THE RATE OF PROFIT TO FALL

Perhaps the central flaw of capitalist economies is that they progress through cycles of boom and bust. Key to this phenomenon is the rate of profit that investors can recover from a business venture. Early classical economists like Adam Smith and David Ricardo who had developed versions of a Labour Theory of Value argued that the rate of profit was determined by market competition:

○ At the start of an economic cycle, labour and capital are idle, so there is little demand. As a result, they can be bought for less than they are worth. This allows investors to make a good return on their investment;

○ New business activity creates employment which raises demand across the economy, encouraging other investors to start new ventures of their own;

○ As the economic cycle progresses, there are fewer workers – particularly those with high skills – left to employ. In order to secure the labour they require, businesses are obliged to offer higher wages and improved conditions. The result is that the cost of the value producing input – labour – increases without a commensurate increase in the surplus value produced;

○ Eventually, labour costs rise to the point that businesses are unable to make sufficient profits to allow them to continue. Businesses close, workers are fired, and a slump occurs.

○ The slump continues until the cost of labour has fallen to the point where businesses begin hiring once more, and the cycle starts again.

Marx took issue with this view, arguing that competition alone did not explain falling profits. According to Marx, technology played a greater role. Individual businesses could gain more of an advantage by replacing workers with machinery. This had the effect of lowering the cost of production. However, by removing the one input that generates value – labour – automation served to lower the amount of surplus value as a whole. Marx acknowledged that this formula did not always work. This was because businesses could adopt other measures to drive up the exploitation of the remaining workers. These might include speeding up the rate of production, extending workers' hours and cutting workers' pay.

At this point, these exceptions to the general rule look more like special pleading. A simpler explanation is that whatever was driving the rate of profit down had relatively little to do with labour and, indeed, that automation may provide an entirely viable means of driving *up* the rate of profit without the need to drive down the price of labour. Contemporary complexity theory offers an alternative – and altogether more plausible – explanation for the tendency for the rate of profit to fall. This is that in any complex system – such as a person, a business or an economy – there is a constant battle to maintain complexity. However, this battle must always overcome two countervailing trends:

○ The tendency for the value of energy to fall

○ The tendency for diminishing returns on technology.

Complexity theory argues that complexity arises in the form of solutions to the problems that these trends give rise to.

However, the paradox is that every "solution" – such as automated production, CFCs or the war on terror – comes with new versions of the same types of problems; but at a greater energy cost.

Remember that for the best part of three centuries, our economies have had access to spare energy. Indeed, it is worth noting that in what was then a small Scottish town, at the same time Adam Smith was labouring away at *The Wealth of Nations*, James Watt was putting the final touches to the first commercial steam engine. As Soddy observes:

> "It is significant to reflect that Glasgow, which produced James Watt, the inventor who brought the steam engine to practical success, was the home of Adam Smith, the father of the system of political economy under which the scientific era has developed. Whilst the former in 1774 was perfecting an engine destined to lift men from the drudgery of animal labour and to establish over the whole world a new mode of livelihood, the latter in 1776 was erecting into a theoretical system the conditions under which, *till then*, men had pursued their economic livelihood. The world might have assimilated either the steam engine or the economics, but it is difficult to understand how it could possibly digest two such mutually incompatible productions simultaneously."

While Smith was concerned with the miniscule additional surplus value that might be squeezed out of a worker, Watt was embarking on the practical means of releasing the massive value boost that humanity had stumbled on in the form of fossil carbon fuels.

While labour – as a form of energy (muscle power) – does provide a small amount of value directly, it is the value that labour serves to harness and focus from fossil fuel that generates profit. And through automation, that harnessing and focussing of energy can be accomplished by machines without the need for human labour at all. So within this energy view of value, a machine that can harness and focus energy is no different in its effect to a human – other than that the machine need not be fed and has no need to sleep.

Why, then, does the rate of profit fall? The answer appears to be twofold:

- ○ Automation comes with diminishing returns. James Watt was able to invent steam engines more or less alone. To invent a jet engine involved teams of engineers and technicians. Leading edge science and engineering today requires university research teams spread across several sites around the planet, and enabled by modern communications infrastructure. Arguably, despite this additional input, the incremental improvements that are returned are smaller at each stage. That is, it costs increasingly more to get back increasingly less. That is, diminishing returns;[7]

- ○ Energy itself comes with diminishing returns. This is the idea of the low hanging fruit principle – we extract

[7] Medical science writer Ben Goldacre makes a similar observation about medical technology. According to Goldacre almost all of the big medical breakthroughs occurred in the years between the synthesis of artificial insulin in 1929 and the first heart transplant in 1969. Since then, medicine has advanced in increments. Goldacre, B. 2009. *Bad Science*. Harper Perennial.

the easiest energy first, and only move on to the more expensive (to recover) energy once this has been exhausted. Offshore oil is more expensive than onshore oil; ultra-deep water oil is more expensive than offshore.

When Marx was writing, there was so much spare coal in Europe and the USA that it was inconceivable that the cost of energy could ever increase to the point that it would have an impact on the economy as a whole. Nevertheless, we know from the history of fossil fuel extraction that this is precisely what has happened. Crucially, it has happened unevenly. That is, there is little – if any – investment in costlier coal, oil or gas extraction while there are still surpluses of cheaper deposits to be had.

Modern oil analysts refer to the way energy investment operates as "the choke chain". A little like walking a dog on a choke-chain lead – if the dog runs too far ahead, the chain collar forces it to stop until its walker catches up again. Rather like the business cycle itself:

○ When a new *recoverable*[8] fossil carbon fuel deposit is found, people will invest to extract it;

○ This provides the wider economy with a new input of relatively cheap energy;

○ This enables profitable investment in new businesses, which brings about a boom in the economy;

[8] In the energy industry, the term "recoverable" refers to a deposit that can be profitably extracted at the prevailing market price.

- Eventually, the economy grows to the point where there is insufficient energy to go around, and the price of energy increases;

- This causes investors to initiate projects to bring even costlier energy into production as this has become recoverable at the higher price;

- Unfortunately, the higher energy price also serves to crush demand, pushing the wider economy into recession. This temporarily "strands" the capital that has already been sunk into new energy recovery;

- Recession results in an over-supply of energy that forces market prices lower than the original extraction cost.

- New businesses utilise this spare energy, and the cycle begins once again;

- Because most of the cost of extraction is up front, once the normal round of bankruptcies and mergers has played out, the cost of the new energy deposits become profitable once more.

For individual businesses, what counts as this cycle plays out is the amount of energy per worker. That is, how much energy can each worker harness and focus to generate surplus value in the form of newly created wealth. New technology coupled to cheap energy allows energy per capita to increase. But as diminishing returns take effect energy per capita drops and the rate of profit falls.

The same process plays out at the macro level. Since 1970, the economies of the developed countries have experienced a decline in energy per capita for the entire population. In the workplace this largely translates into falling productivity.

Some of the fall in per capita energy use is explained through energy efficient technology; although most of these gains were made in the 1980s, and we have experienced diminishing returns since then. To add to this problem, so-called conventional (i.e. cheap) crude oil peaked in 2005 (Britain's North Sea fields actually peaked in 1999, and are now producing just a third of their peak production). This had not stopped global oil production from rising. However, as conventional crude oil production falls, the difference has to be made up by unconventional (i.e. expensive) deposits such as oil shale, tar sands, ultra-deep water and Arctic, that are far more expensive to produce.

Our understanding of this process is obscured by the role of energy at the societal level and by the way money operates as a medium of exchange. These both produce additional pressures on profits that serve to further distort both business and choke chain cycles. Most obviously, states depend upon the revenue from taxation to operate. But this tends to lead them to attempt to increase taxation and cut spending at the point when profitability and energy investment are lowest. That is, they tend to exacerbate the problem. Less obviously, because almost all of our money is *borrowed* into existence, the pressure to repay debts is highest during recessions. This means that paying existing debt while refusing further credit also served to depress an already slumping economy.

Money, then, adds another layer of complexity to the puzzle of value. But despite the importance of money to the way economies operate few economics courses take the time to examine what money is or where it comes from. This renders economists and political decision makers as ignorant and mistaken about money as the general public at large.

THE RELATIONSHIP OF MONEY TO ENERGY [9]

centre. We access it across the internet or via plastic cards, which we may occasionally use to obtain currency from an ATM machine. This currency in the form of bank notes is also an abstraction. You can neither feed nor clothe yourself with bank notes. Rather, these notes, plastic cards and computer bytes are a *representation* of wealth and an abstracted measure of value. Indeed, even the coins that most economies use for small change are merely tokens today. The metal and energy used in their manufacture are a mere fraction of their monetary value.

It was not always this way. The earliest "money" consisted of pieces of precious metals like gold and silver that were broken from bars to make a transaction. Later, states developed mints to strike coins of equal weight; removing the need to weigh money during a transaction. The king or emperor's head would be stamped into the coin as a guarantee of its worth. Laws were enacted to oblige traders to accept the money, and insisting that it be used for the payment of taxes.

There are good reasons for using gold and silver as a measure of value:

- ○ They are inert, meaning that they endure over time without oxidising and decaying

- ○ They are rare, and so protect against inflation

- ○ Until recently, they were not used for manufactured goods other than jewellery

[9] For a more detailed explanation of debt-based money and its impacts, see: Watkins, T. 2016. *The Root of All Evil: The problem of debt-based money.* Waye Forward publishing.

○ They require more energy than other metals to extract, refine and produce.

It is this last category that makes them useful as money, because it allows them to be a measurable and convertible store of value. That is, if we know how many socially necessary mega joules it takes to produce an ounce of gold, then we have a yardstick against which the socially necessary mega joules required to produce any other good or service can be measured.

In practice the value of gold as money can be distorted through supply and demand in exactly the way in which supply and demand can impact upon any good or service. This was most dramatically illustrated when the Spanish Empire sought to expand its wealth by plundering the massive gold and silver reserves of South and Central America. The result was not the economic boom that they anticipated. On the contrary, they generated an inflation that threw the European economy into chaos, and ultimately brought about the demise of their Empire. Why? Because there was insufficient unused energy and wealth in Europe to be mobilised by the new influx of money. As a result, all the additional gold and silver served to do was to raise the price of the wealth and energy that was already in use. That is, it created inflation in the same way as modern government money printing often causes inflation.

Abstracted currency causes even greater difficulty because it is even harder to use it as a measure of energy content; i.e. value. Imagine you had a small economy with a money supply of 10 ounces of gold. In ideal conditions (which never exist in the real world) at any moment you could only use this gold to mobilise the energy equivalent – either as embodied energy (i.e. capital) or as work (energy). The circulation – or "velocity" – of the gold would allow the economy to mobilise much more energy and capital. Nevertheless, the gold limit would serve to limit economic activity to the capital and energy which the gold could mobilise.

There is a problem, however. Throughout human history we have generally (localised famines aside) had access to far more energy than we have had gold to measure it with. Indeed, the modern global economy could not operate on the energy equivalent of all of the gold we currently have available – unless, of course we pretend that the value of an ounce of gold is far greater than it really is. In practice – but not by design – that is exactly what we have done. Throughout our history we have developed ways of abstracting money so that we can pretend that there is far more value in our currency than is actually the case.

The first banknotes were created as receipts for an amount of gold or silver coins deposited at the bank. Indeed, even today, paper currencies around the world contain the promise to pay the bearer some notional value. The British pound sterling began as a receipt for a pound (in weight) of sterling silver. The first US dollar notes printed by the Federal Reserve could be exchanged for a genuine silver dollar.

Having to take the first banknotes – those issued by private banks – to the bank in order to get gold and silver coins to make transactions was a lot of hassle. More often than not, people chose to simply swap the notes directly. This gave rise to the second[10] form of banking fraud. Observing that very few people ever turned up at the bank to retrieve their gold, banks began to print more banknotes than there was gold on deposit. So long as this new currency was able to mobilise energy and capital, it would not be obvious. Indeed, it might even result in an economic boom. However, once the currency was over-printed, the result was inflation. When inflation set in, traders began to ask for payment in gold. Depositors went to the bank to recover their gold, only to find that there was not enough to go around. In the 1840s, the overproduction of banknotes by English banks led to a financial crisis that was only halted by the British government borrowing £2 million in gold from France. To prevent this from occurring in future, the government introduced the Bank Charter Act of 1844, which made the issuing of private currency a criminal offense.

The third form of bank fraud arose with the development of cheque accounts as an alternative to the now illegal practice of issuing private banknotes. Again, most likely the result of customer convenience, it was far easier for traders and consumers to swap paper cheques than to go to the bank to withdraw cash. It also created a system in which the transfer of currency became even more abstracted. The bank no longer had to move money around in a vault. With a cheque

[10] The first form of fraud was the practice of adulterating the precious metal content of coins; for example by adding base metals or by reducing the weight of the coins by snipping or filing (one of the reasons why even today, coins have milled edges). This practice often brought down kingdoms and empires, and accounted for the heads of more than a few emperors and kings.

account system, customer accounts and transactions between them could simply be recorded as transfers on the bank's ledger book.

This system gave rise to national systems of fractional reserve banking. Governments would hold an amount of gold equivalent to the notes and coins that they printed. These would be distributed into the banking system via the central bank. The central bank would enforce a reserve ratio – a proportion of the notes and coins they would have to hold on deposit when they made loans. Because the loans themselves were merely changes to the ledger book, banks could lend more money than they actually had. For example, on a reserve ratio of ten to one, a bank could lend out £1,000 for every £100 it held on deposit. Again, provided that the additional currency loaned into circulation could mobilise the equivalent *spare* energy and capital, the result would be an economic upswing.

But there was a sting in the tail of fractional reserve banking. Whereas the early banknotes had been merely *exchanged* into existence against an equivalent amount of gold, chequebook currency is *loaned* into existence. And this means that at any time there is never enough currency in existence to pay off the original loan with interest. So where does the interest come from? It can come from just two sources. Either governments must print the equivalent of the interest in the form of new notes and coins – something governments almost never do – or banks must continue to grow the amount of currency they loan into existence. So an economy based on fractional reserve banking is like a game of musical chairs – so long as the music keeps playing (i.e. banks keep lending) the game goes on. But when the music stops, there are not enough chairs for everyone – companies and households go bust and the economy falls into a depression.

There is a less obvious added complication with fractional reserve banking. The system feeds on itself. Initially economic cycles can begin because there is excess energy and capital lying idle. Workers are unemployed, machinery stands silent, raw resources remain in the ground, and there are plenty of recoverable reserves of coal, gas and oil. With some entrepreneurial thinking and the backing of a prudent loan from the bank, a smart businessperson can get a new enterprise up and running. The newly created employment bolsters demand in the broader economy. The banks begin to notice that things are picking up, and start to lend to other businesses. Pretty soon, the economy is booming once again, and all of that excess capital and energy has been deployed. At this point, you would anticipate inflation. But the inflation does not manifest as a general increase in prices across the board. The initial inflation is limited to particular asset classes whose price far exceeds their value. In the modern world we are used to asset bubbles (i.e. inflation) in property and shares. But almost anything can become the subject of an asset bubble. For example, in Holland in the 1630s, surplus currency generated a bubble in tulip bulbs. As demand for tulip bulbs increased, so the price shot up. It became possible to take out a loan from the bank to buy tulip bulbs and then sell them on at a profit. The trouble is that there comes a point where everyone who can borrow to purchase the asset *has* borrowed to purchase the asset. At that point there are no more buyers and the bubble bursts. The asset does not simply return to its true (energy) value, but drops to zero.

When a bubble bursts, it leaves a massive volume of unpaid and unpayable debts. There are only two ways in which these can be managed. Either the government must use a proportion of future taxation to take over the debt or businesses and households must simply be allowed to default, with the losses falling collectively on their creditors. A potential third way of removing the debt involves the modern version of what early civilisations called "debt jubilees". The idea is that the government would use its power to print money in order to pay off outstanding debt. The thinking behind this is that both the new money and the debt would cancel each other out, and would thus not create inflation. However, to implement such an approach would involve a huge cultural shift in the way people think about money and debt.

Many people today assume that we still have a system of fractional reserve banking. This is wrong. Today, the relationship between private and central banks has been reversed. The central bank no longer sets a limit on the amount of loans that a bank can make. On the contrary, central banks exist in the modern world solely to print or borrow money into existence to prevent bank runs. Banks themselves are free to loan into existence as much new money as they can get away with.

This is the fourth form of bank fraud. In the late 1980s, computerisation allowed banks to deploy securitisation. The idea behind this was simple enough. In earlier times, a bank would make a loan in exchange for a promise and a claim on an asset. That is, if you went to the bank to ask for a mortgage, you would sign a mortgage agreement. This was your promise. The agreement would also include a clause that allowed the bank to repossess your home in the event that you could not keep up with the payments. The bank would make a lot more money back from you than they loaned you to begin with. However, this would only accrue over 20 to 30 years. Banks could make money by making lots of loans. But they could not afford to risk making loans to people who might not be able to repay. So banks tended to be small, local (because they needed to know their customers) and conservative.

Securitisation shifted the balance of risk. What it allowed banks to do was to distribute risk by creating a "derivative". Essentially, they would package a proportion of the income from all of the different loans that they had made into a new investment vehicle. The advantage of this was that it minimised risk. For example, a bank might know that statistically five percent of loans will go bad – but it does not know which five. If, on the other hand, it takes one percent of the income from each of one hundred loans, and then repackages these into 100 new securitised investment vehicles, it can distribute the risk. Instead of having to wait to get their money back, banks could make money selling these securities to investors.

The problem is that like all "solutions," securitisation came with unforeseen consequences. Whereas banks used to make their money from the loans that they issued, with securitisation they could make far more money from selling the securities on to investors. Whereas they might have to wait 25 years to get the full income from a mortgage, they could get their money back immediately from selling a security. And securities were standardised. The risks could be measured and their value calculated. This made them to all intents and purposes a new form of currency similar – but even more abstracted – in their way to the banknotes and cheques of earlier times. The nature of banking changed too. Whereas banks had been small, local and conservative, in the course of a decade or two they grew into global behemoths. And everyone wanted in on the deal. Building societies effectively bribed their members to allow them to become banks so that they could get a piece of the action. Commercial banks moved onto the high street even as high street banks muscled their way into commercial lending.

Whereas banknote fraud had led to local bank runs, and cheque account fraud created national crises, a run on derivatives had the potential to affect the entire global economy. Nor did it stop there. The 1980s and 1990s had seen another ramp up in global energy availability following the oil shocks of the 1973 OPEC embargo and the 1979 Iran/Iraq war. Investment in the 1970s (when prices were high) brought new fields such as the North Sea into production in the 1980s. Once again, there was plenty of spare energy and capital to deploy. As the economy took off in the 1990s, the banks wanted even more of the action. But there was a problem. There are only so many responsible and credit worthy borrowers out there. And much as the banks wanted to lend, they were beginning to run out of trustworthy borrowers to offer loans to. So they did what every other crook and fraudster has done down the ages – they adulterated the new currency. Instead of slipping just five percent of bad loans into what should have been standardised securities, they began to throw in a handful of riskier loans as well. Because the economy was booming, they got away with it. So they issued even more risky loans. But just to be on the safe side, they took out insurance to cover the expected income from these securities. Then they got the ratings agencies to stamp them as Triple-A rated.

With the boom in full swing, the banks were desperate to find new borrowers. An army of freelance mortgage brokers were deployed on the front lines, lending money to just about anyone that they could vaguely claim was credit worthy. When even this failed, and the value of the securities began to slip, the banks set up special offshore investment companies to buy their own securities solely to keep accelerating the price. And as happens in all bubbles, as the feeding frenzy reached its peak, investors within the banks began to buy these so-called "assets."

The sub-prime mortgage bubble eventually burst because the price of oil spiked in 2006. Global oil production had flattened in 2005. In effect there was insufficient spare energy to allow the boom of the 1990s and early 2000s to continue. Central banks acted according to neoclassical economic theory and hiked interest rates in order to dampen down demand to prevent oil prices translating into generalised inflation. Sub-prime borrowers that had been just about managing on low monthly interest rates were suddenly plunged into arrears. House prices plummeted, and many people in the USA simply posted the keys to their homes to the banks and walked away. As the income from the loans disappeared, the securities that were derived from them also failed. The banks turned to the insurers to cover the shortfall. But like all insurers, they never had sufficient money to cover the losses if all securities failed at the same time. Like all bubble assets, the price of securities fell to zero.

In 2008, the banks claimed that they had a liquidity crisis. That is, they claimed that they had assets on their books the value of which would more than cover the debts that they owed to each other and to their creditors. It was just that they were unable to liquidate these assets at short notice. And so the world came to think of 2008 as a "credit crunch". The solution to a credit crunch – effectively a cash-flow problem – was for governments to give the banks the money they needed to settle their short-term debts, with a view to taking the money back once the banks got back on their feet.

The banks lied of course. There never were assets to cover their obligations. The banks were sat on pieces of paper that were no more valuable that a 200 million mark note at the height of the inflation in Weimar Germany in 1923. But by getting governments to give them the money needed to bail them out, they had committed the final fraud of banking.

Where did governments get the money to bail out the banks? They borrowed it. Who did they borrow it from? Form the banks of course. Whereas, when they issue loans to you and me they end up with a piece of paper that says "Joe Bloggs will repay the loan;" when they loaned money to governments, they had a piece of paper signed by the governor of the central bank that said "I promise to pay the bearer on demand…" That is, the banks had obtained money as good as the money that governments issue. And what makes this money so good is that it is founded upon the backs of future taxpayers in perpetuity.

This has been a particular problem for countries that do not have their own currency; such as the member states in the Eurozone. Countries like the UK and USA have the luxury of – within limits – being able to borrow or print money in order to inflate away their debts. Countries like Portugal and Greece have no such luxury. All they are able to do is perpetually repackage their debts; effectively condemning future generations to poverty. But even sovereign – i.e. independent – currencies cannot be inflated away forever.

Remember how each form of banking ultimately comes to an end. The economy reaches a point where it has far exceeded its available capital and energy. It has succeeded in keeping the ball rolling by pumping up asset bubbles and using price inflation to maintain demand. But without a new spare energy source, the system has to crash. This raises a key question today. Can we secure the energy required to produce sufficient new wealth into the economy for future taxpayers to repay the money that our governments borrowed to bail out the banks? The full amount of this debt today amounts to more than six times the value of all of the wealth in existence. This poses some interesting existential crises:

- Can we generate the wealth required without incurring additional borrowing that would defeat the object of the exercise?

- Assuming we can, is it possible to find six times the energy and resources that we currently have access to in order to create the new wealth?

- And if we can, will our ecosystem be able to cope with the additional pollution and heat that this wealth creation must inevitably involve?

In reality, the volume of currency in existence is now so abstracted from the value that it is meant to represent that it all but impossible to prevent the entire global banking system from collapsing... it is just a matter of time. Even central bankers today talk in terms of "extend and pretend." That is, continue pumping liquidity into the banking system while bolstering public confidence and desperately hoping that smart people will be able to figure out how to unwind the mess.

HOW SURPLUS VALUE IS STOLEN

Once we see that it is energy rather than labour (or indeed food) that is the source of value, we begin to see the lie in the belief that capitalists somehow steal the surplus value generated by workers. In an ideal situation, both actually trade wealth for wealth in the process of production. That is, the capitalists provide wealth in the form of the embodied energy contained in the buildings, machinery, tools and raw materials that they bring to the productive process. Similarly, workers bring wealth in the form of their skills and their time. And while they also bring a tiny amount of energy in the form of muscle power, this is far too little to create the surplus that accrues at the end of the process. Only the massive energy content of the fuels – which cost a tiny fraction of the value they generate – can produce surplus value.

We might argue about the relative share of the surplus that goes to capitalists and workers. Certainly there are many occasions where workers are under-paid while capitalists walk away with more than their fair share. However, in the grand scheme of things, this type of argument is largely a fight over the scraps while the real thieves are ignored entirely; or at best treated as being no different to capitalists.

The real thieves are those who benefit from the productive process without putting any wealth in to begin with. That is, the people who really do get something for nothing out of the productive process. It would be tempting to refer to these people as "the bankers;" but this would be to over-simplify. As we have seen, banks create currency out of thin air when they make loans. That currency comes with the big string of compound interest attached. The result is that banks do not simply provide us with the currency we need; they *rent* it to us.

This is different to the way other goods – e.g. cars, houses and tools – are rented. In those cases, some wealth belonging to the owner is transferred to the borrower. But in the case of banking, no wealth is transferred. Rather, the borrower is given an entirely fraudulent claim on the wealth of others. And in the process a tiny fraction of the value of all of the other currency in the system is stolen (through inflation). In ordinary circumstances, the rate of inflation is low enough that we do not notice the theft. However, look back over a few years and it is clear that many of life's necessities appear to have increased in price – in reality, it is not the goods that have appreciated, but the currency that has depreciated.

So banks steal wealth from everyone else when they issue new money. But they also steal wealth at the end of the process of production by insisting that true capitalists pay interest upon the wealth-free currency that was extended at the start. That is, the banks take a share – indeed, a large share – of surplus value to which they are not entitled.

Nor does it end with businesses paying back loans. In order to guarantee that businesses can grow sufficiently to continue meeting the payments on their debts, banks must also loan currency – again created out of thin air – to households so that they can buy the goods that businesses make. And again, these loans come with compound interest, so that workers must give up a large part of their share of the surplus value generated from cheap energy in order to pay back their loans.

Unfortunately, it is not just some separate class of bankers who are parasitically feeding on the productive process. Anyone who has a pension, insurance or a savings account also has a stake in this fraud. Moreover, modern businesses have grown up in an economy in which debt precedes profit. The result is that they cannot afford simply to pay back debts and run on day-to-day income. This is why governments felt that they had no choice but to bail out the banks in 2008. Aside from the immediate impact of a banking collapse on our ability to make payments and to withdraw cash, had the banks been allowed to fail, savers and pensioners would have lost everything. Insurance companies would have failed with the result that households and businesses would no longer be protected. Mortgage holders would have lost their homes, leaving the state to pick up the bill for widespread homelessness.

We can argue about the means by which governments have attempted – and probably failed – to save the banks. However, it is hard to claim that governments should have simply allowed banks to fail because we can do without them.

Obviously, some people benefit from banking far more than others. Those who own shares in the banks themselves enjoy a much greater share of the surplus value that our economy generates than does, for example, the average pensioner. Similarly, the owners of the assets – e.g. property, fine art, corporate and government bonds – whose price is inflated as asset bubbles inflate benefit far more than the average saver. So what is needed is a means of protecting ordinary savers and pensioners, while allowing shareholders and asset speculators to reap the full effect of the risks they took. Unfortunately, the quantitative easing policy has the very opposite impact – it enriches the already rich while undermining the income to savers and pensioners.

Several potential alternatives have been mooted. However, these will only succeed if they change the way money works. For all of the fancy terms that modern bankers employ to disguise the theft, debt-based electronic currency is merely a more sophisticated version of the chequebook fraud, banknote fraud and adulterated coinage fraud of times gone by. The harms are the same. The only difference is the scale at which the harms take their toll.

Only a money creation system that is based on sacrificed wealth will solve the problem. That is, nobody within the productive process should be allowed to get something for nothing. Just as capitalists bring the wealth embodied in capital and the workers bring their time and skills to the productive process, so banks should be forced to bring only real wealth. That is, everyone who wishes to take a share of the surplus value generated from cheap energy must first give something up.

As an essential first step, states *must* take back the sole power to create money. In effect, this would force banks to operate in the way most people – including economists and politicians – think that they operate anyway. That is, banks should only be able to lend real money that they have on deposit from savers and investors.

However, this alone is insufficient because there is nothing to stop politicians from simply printing currency to pay for the rash promises they make during elections. Some means of linking money to its true energy value is essential to a functioning monetary system. For centuries, gold and silver have served this purpose. This is because these metals are rare and require considerable energy (i.e. value) to produce. As such, they can act as a proxy for energy.

Unfortunately, there is reason to believe that this will not help us meet the challenges facing us. This is because we no longer have access to abundant cheap energy. As we shall see, the twin challenges of climate change-imposed energy denial, and the gradual loss of abundant cheap fossil carbon fuels, leaves us facing a future of declining energy. In monetary terms, this means that even a gold-backed currency will lose its value simply because it can no longer mobilise spare energy.

It may be that in future we will need to link money directly to energy. That is, that the amount of energy we generate at any time will determine the amount of money in circulation. This would no doubt be unpopular because – unlike artificial austerity policies – it really would oblige us to live within our means. However, in the longer term it would force us to take responsibility for our children and grandchildren's future – because it would oblige us to generate sufficient clean energy to pay for any consumption we may wish to engage in.

PART II:
CONSEQUENCES

CONTEMPORARY PREDICAMENTS

Banking failures result from a collision between abstracted currency systems and the real material world. The few economists who were alert enough to see the 2008 crash coming expressed this through a "Debt to GDP ratio". While mainstream economists had worried about the ratio of government debt to GDP, the more prescient economists had spotted that the ratio of *private* (i.e. household and corporate) debt to GDP was more important because this accounted for far more of the abstracted currency that banks had been loaning into the system:

UK Money Supply 1870-2010, (£ billions)

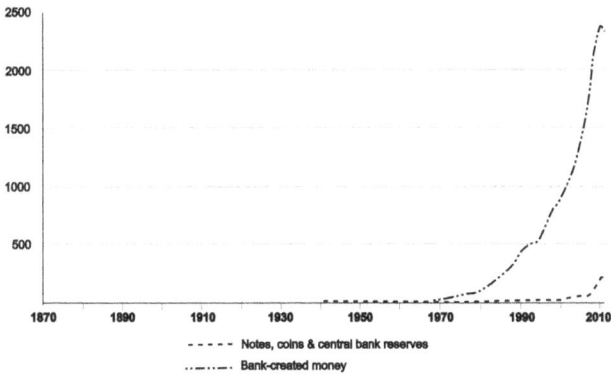

- - - - - Notes, coins & central bank reserves
..—..—. Bank-created money

UK PERSONAL DEBT (1993 TO 2012) £ BILLIONS

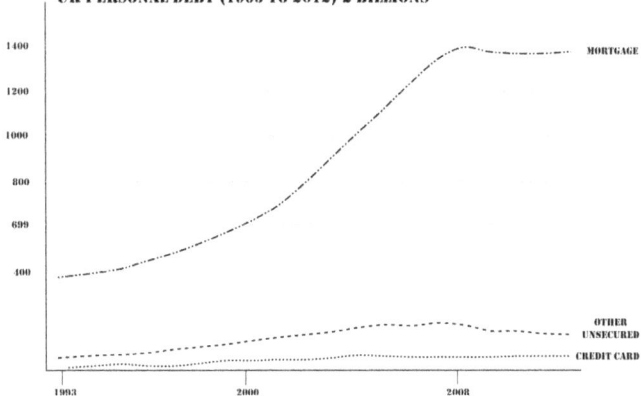

MORTGAGE

OTHER UNSECURED

CREDIT CARD

Like gold, GDP is only an imperfect measure of the energy and capital used in an economy. It is a flawed measure insofar as it measures national economic activity in a globalised economy; and because some inflated asset (bubble) purchases also appear in the figure. Nevertheless, GDP is a useful back-of-an-envelope representation of the energy deployed in an economy. So when the ratio of debt to GDP grows too wide over too short a period – i.e. when available energy and capital stall but abstracted currency continues to grow – the result is always a crash.

The means of recovering from a crash are well enough understood. First, we have to write off outstanding debt in order to align the currency with energy once more. Second, we have to utilise additional spare energy and capital to get the economy growing again. Some combination of these actions is what has revived economies throughout history. But this may not be possible today.

Our industrial economy is based on burning fossil carbon – the stored solar energy of millions of years' worth of plant growth. The consequences of burning all of this carbon, and releasing carbon dioxide and other greenhouse gases into the atmosphere are becoming all too clear. Global temperatures are rising remorselessly. Weather patterns are shifting. Ecosystems are dying. Icecaps and glaciers are melting. Sea levels are rising. In short, the very life support systems that underpin human existence on the planet are threatened. And even if humanity survives, the global economy most certainly will not.

To take just one of the threats that face us: 85 percent of the cities on earth were – for good economic reasons – built on coasts or tidal estuaries. These are now at risk from several metres of sea level rise that at best will occur after 2100, but at worse may happen as early as 2050. Long before then, however, major centres of the global economy such as London and New York will already be so compromised that it is doubtful whether they will be able to function in their current roles. The result is that trillions of pounds/dollars of capital investment will become worthless. In less important towns and cities along America's eastern seaboard, we can already see the future. In Miami Beach, for example, city streets regularly experience so-called "sunny day floods" as high tides push sea water in through storm drains that are now below sea level.

To meet the targets agreed in Paris in 2015, the developed countries need to stop burning fossil carbon immediately. There is absolutely no sign that this is going to happen or, in reality, that even those who claim to care about climate change are prepared to compromise their lifestyles to the extent needed. So we may well drive ourselves extinct. Whatever we do, we are now guaranteed to leave our children and grandchildren to inherit the industrial equivalent of scorched earth; most likely in the form of a compromised food chain and the inevitability of widespread famine. Just like the many thousands of lifeforms that our lifestyles are currently driving to extinction, humans also have a habitat that requires a particular temperature. And if you don't believe that a two degree increase in that temperature is going to have a serious impact, just remember how you felt last time you got ill and your temperature rose by two or three degrees.

Our predicament is that the damage we could inflict on ourselves if we were to cease burning fossil carbon immediately may be even more life-threatening than the short-term impact of climate change. If you wanted to produce a famine, I can think of nothing more calculated a way of doing so than to halt all of the commercial vehicle journeys in the developed world, where most of the countries have little more than three days' worth of food at any time. In the USA, the average food item travels 3,000 miles between the farm and the plate. In Europe the mileage is better, but not so much so that we are in any position to ramp up local food deliveries.

The common response to objections to cutting fossil carbon consumption is that we can shift to renewable energy. This is an interesting psychological sedative. However, it is not grounded in reality.[11] While we undoubtedly should replace coal and gas-fired power stations with wind, solar, tidal and hydroelectric generation, we have to recognise that these are only a means of shifting the way we produce electricity. And at present, with the exception of hydroelectricity, they produce just a tiny fraction of our total energy consumption.

[11] That it is *theoretically* possible or even *technically* possible (which many dispute) to develop an economy powered entirely upon renewables is neither here nor there. What matters is whether we have sufficient spare energy, raw materials, labour and capital to achieve this herculean project.

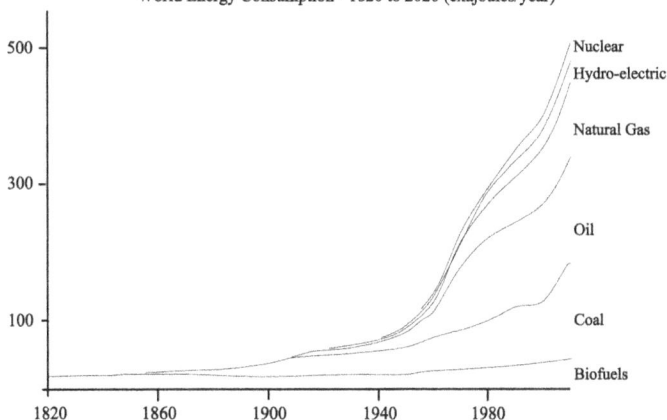

World Energy Consumption - 1820 to 2020 (exajoules/year)

Electricity accounts for just 20-25 percent of the energy we consume. The other 75-80 percent is evenly split between the energy we use to heat and cool our buildings and to power our agriculture and industry; and the energy we use to transport ourselves and our goods around the planet. So even if we were to shift all of our electricity generation to renewables – something that would require a herculean effort and more capital investment than is currently available – we would still only have replaced 20-25 percent of the fossil carbon that we need to stop burning immediately.

We might, of course shift to electric vehicles and switch to electric heaters and cookers in the home. But this is only likely to shave another five percent off our fossil carbon consumption. And again, to bring about this shift rapidly will involve a herculean effort and more capital than is currently available. In practice, the most effective means of lowering our fossil carbon consumption is simply to voluntarily lower our consumption. Simply turning off

71

electrical appliances, insulating walls and roofs, installing double glazing and turning the thermostat down can save the energy equivalent of the proposed Hinkley Point C nuclear power station.

Unfortunately, transport is the elephant in the room that nobody wants to talk about. It is true that we now have some very impressive electric cars and scooters that offer better performance and far cheaper running costs than conventional cars and motorcycles. With government intervention to expand the recharging infrastructure and to encourage us (perhaps through a scrappage scheme) to switch, we could make the transition within a decade.[12] But this only explains how we are going to move ourselves around. It does nothing to address the freight problem.

All of the goods and services that we consume begin with global scale mineral extraction. This is now conducted on so great a scale that it depends on gargantuan diesel powered machinery and trucks to extract and move metal ore. Most metal smelting processes depend upon heat far in excess of that which can be produced using renewable electricity generation. And once the metal is produced, it has to be transported on diesel powered ships and trucks to the factory where it will be turned into finished goods. These finished goods will, in turn, be loaded onto trucks, ships and trucks again to get them to the end consumers.

So far, nobody has come up with a realistic means of powering machinery, ships and trucks – still less air freight

[12] My own view is that insofar as we shift to electric vehicles, it will be through the growth of driverless cars and Uber-like taxi services coupled to a big decline (in urban areas) in car ownership.

– using anything other than oil. With time, energy and capital that we not have, we might rebuild, extend and fully electrify our rail networks in order to cut back our need for shipping and trucks. However, the last mile or so of every journey will continue to require trucks that, for the time being, have to run on diesel.

This may leave us facing a double-whammy. Because while we may decide to continue burning fossil carbon to prevent a collapse of the global economy, there may be physical limits on further fossil carbon consumption that relate directly to value.

In Marx's formulation of the Labour Theory of Value, the basic idea was that to have profit (surplus value) one of the inputs to the productive process must be paid less than the value that it generates. Marx said that this input was labour. Workers were paid what was required for them to maintain and refresh themselves. But this was only a fraction of the value that they added. While there is a certain truth to this, the difference is minimal. Human beings simply cannot produce anything like the energy (work) that would have been required to generate the surplus value of the Industrial Revolution. Nor, indeed, could the slave trade that preceded – and provided the seed capital for – industrialisation.

It was coal that generated almost all of the surplus value of the Industrial Revolution. Coal was cheap because it was easy to obtain, but it provided vast amounts of energy in return. Once coal was combined with increasingly efficient steam engines, the modern world became possible. But coal does not stay cheap. Remember that the people of Coalbrookdale (the clue is in the name) could simply chop coal from exposed seams. But this easy coal was soon used up by the growing iron industry. People were obliged to dig ever deeper and deploy ever more energy-intensive technologies to allow them to continue to extract the growing supplies demanded by a fast expanding industrial economy. On the other side of the equation, scientists and engineers continued to discover new uses for coal – such as steel works, railways and steam ships – that continued to pump up demand. Government, too, began to depend upon the tax receipts from coal-powered industry to meet its spending and to service its borrowing.

For the most part, we tend to look to energy *prices* rather than costs when considering profitability. However, while price refers to abstracted currency, it is cost that mirrors value most closely. Cost in this sense is a measure of energy input rather than monetary investment. So that while we can temporarily shift prices around, since we cannot bend the laws of thermodynamics, the energy cost of obtaining energy is largely beyond human control.

At its simplest, we understand that it cost far less *energy* to hammer a steel pipe 70 feet into the ground in Pennsylvania in the 1860s, than it currently costs in energy to drill through a mile of rock that is itself beneath three miles of water. Similarly, it cost far less energy for the good folk in the Severn valley to fetch cart loads of coal from the nearby hills than it costs to dynamite the tops off Appalachian Mountains to access the coal seams beneath.

Scientists such as Charles Hall and David Murphy are currently engaged in work that attempts to provide an accurate measure of these differences in a calculation of

Energy Return on Investment or EROI. The difficulty with this field of work at present is that scientists do not agree upon the point at which energy can be considered to be "returned". For example, should the EROI of oil be calculated at the wellhead, the refinery, the filling station or the engine that burns it? As Charles Hall explains, an EROI of 1:1 would allow you to look at oil at the wellhead; you would need 2:1 to get it to the refinery and 3:1 to put it in your car. But even consumption may not fully capture what is going on, because many governments around the world have built their social structures around the tax-take from oil.

However we eventually come to measure EROI, what is clear is that the trend is remorselessly downward. This is inevitable since competition in a market economy causes extractive industries to go after the cheapest resource first. Nobody in the nineteenth century would have built a deep mine if their competitors could simply hack coal off the side of a neighbouring hill. And nobody today would seriously see Arctic oil extraction as a viable commercial possibility if there were any land-based oil fields still to be developed. This is the tendency for the rate of energy profit to fall. And it is currently irreversible. Whereas the nineteenth century oil industry could recover more than 100 barrels of oil for every barrel-equivalent expended, so-called "unconventional" processes such as hydraulic fracturing and tar sands mining provide returns of less than 10:1 (some commentators even claim tar sands oil has an EROI of less than 3:1). Biodiesel from corn has a negative EROI (it takes more energy to produce than it gives back in return).

This presents a serious question for economists – at what EROI does a modern, globalised, industrial economy become unviable? Obviously there must be such a point, since if every form of energy on the planet had an EROI of 1:1, our entire economy would have to be dedicated solely to producing energy. While we cannot be sure of the point at which modern societies will break down, we can be sure that somewhere between where we are now and an EROI 1:1 will mark the point at which our economy is unviable.

In an early attempt to indicate where this point may lie, Hall produced a hierarchy of societal energy needs similar to Maslow's hierarchy of individual needs. According to this model, the lower the EROI, the more of our way of life we begin to lose. The arts break down at an EROI of 14:1; healthcare at 12:1; food at 5:1:

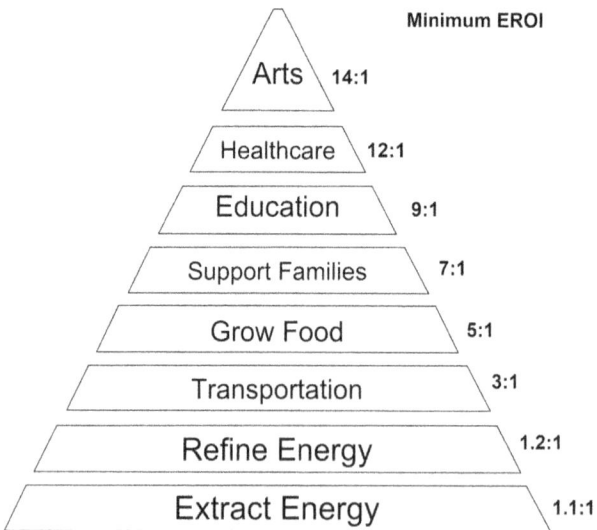

	Minimum EROI
Arts	14:1
Healthcare	12:1
Education	9:1
Support Families	7:1
Grow Food	5:1
Transportation	3:1
Refine Energy	1.2:1
Extract Energy	1.1:1

This in turn raises issues about the proposed alternative and renewable energy generation that might replace fossil carbon. Across their lifespan, wind turbines have an EROI of around 20:1. Rooftop solar PV can produce 12:1 in optimum conditions; although 5:1 is more realistic. Indeed, even in deserts, engineers have experienced EROI-limiting problems caused by heat haze and dust. Nuclear power from pressurised water reactors comes in at 15:1. In contrast, conventional oil and gas in some regions is still in excess of 40:1 while coal is greater than 30:1:[13]

> "Declining EROI is probably already having a large impact on the world economy. As oil and gas provide roughly 60–65% of the world's energy, this will likely have enormous economic consequences for many national economies."

The problem in terms of economic value is that energy does not stop with the resource. In 2006, the US Federal Reserve was undoubtedly correct to fear that a rise in the price of oil would result in generalised inflation. This is simply because everything that we do depends upon energy. So if the cost of recovering energy (EROI) increases, this generates a multiplier effect throughout the economy. For example, an increase in the cost of oil will most obviously be felt as an increase in fuel prices at the pump. However, it will also impact on the price of goods that have to be transported for sale. So it is not simply the case that the end consumer must divert spending to cover increased fuel costs; rather,

[13] Hall, et al. 2014. "EROI of different fuels and the implications for society." *Energy Policy*. Volume 64, January 2014, Pages 141–152.

discretionary spending as a whole will be reduced as all non-discretionary costs (e.g. food, rent/mortgage, clothing, heating, etc) increase in price.

This is the way Marx's "crisis of overproduction" plays out. The global economy depends upon marginal discretionary spending for its existence. That is, it relies on each of us spending a proportion of our income on non-essential consumption so that – across the economy as a whole – there is sufficient demand to maintain growth. When energy costs increase, all of us shift spending from discretionary to non-discretionary items. For the poor, this is most obvious because all non-essential spending disappears. But even the wealthiest will have an imperceptibly small shift away from discretionary spending. For individuals this may seem trivial – one less meal at a restaurant, one less drive to the seaside, one less movie from Netflix, etc. But when all of us across the consuming regions of the global economy do the same thing, the result is collapsing demand and a stagnating economy.

Falling EROI creates the very opposite problem to the one that "peak oil" theorists like Marion King Hubbert thought would occur as we burned our way through the Earth's finite oil deposits. Hubbert was a brilliant geologist employed by Shell to determine how much more oil they could expect to recover from their holdings in the USA. What Hubbert discovered was unnerving. Oil *discoveries* had peaked in the 1930s. Given the rate of extraction and allowing for technical improvements, Hubbert calculated that mainland US oil production would peak around 1970.

When Hubbert went public with his projections he was largely ridiculed by an industry and mass media that simply could not contemplate the idea that one day – and not that far away – their industry would enter a terminal decline. When 1970 came around, the media and industry figures revisited Hubbert's claims once more; pointing out that far from the predicted catastrophe, the USA was producing more oil than ever before. But Hubbert was correct. US oil production had peaked. Even today's fracking boom has failed (although only just) to push production up to the 1970 level.

However, peak oil theorists at the time tended to look solely at the geology. As a result, they assumed that production would follow a bell curve as the resource was used up. Initially, production would grow exponentially. Then, as the half-way point was reached, production would slow, reach a plateau, and then begin to fall away. Most assumed that when this occurred, the result would be the kind of fuel shortages seen in 1973 as a consequence of the OPEC oil embargo or in the UK in 2000 as a result of the fuel protests.

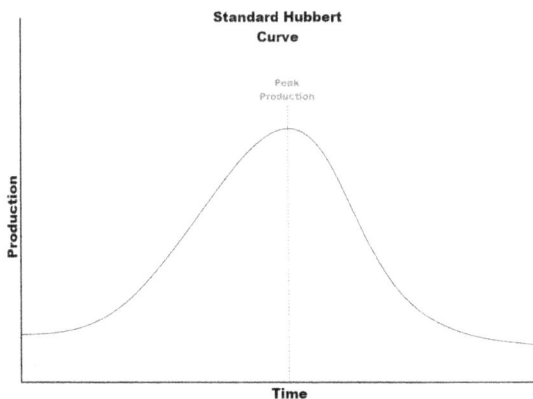

Standard Hubbert Curve

However, energy economists pointed to an alternative consequence. Oil fields on the US mainland had been *allowed* to decline naturally because there were easily recoverable reserves elsewhere. However, when global production as a whole begins to reach a peak, far more effort (energy) will be channelled into recovering what is left in order to keep the supply growing. As available supplies fall, prices will become volatile. Periods of high prices will stimulate investment in the recovery of reserves that would be unprofitable at a lower price. This would create not a bell curve, but what is known as a "Seneca cliff" in which a part of the resource on the downside of the curve is brought forward by higher prices and improved technology in order to maintain growth.

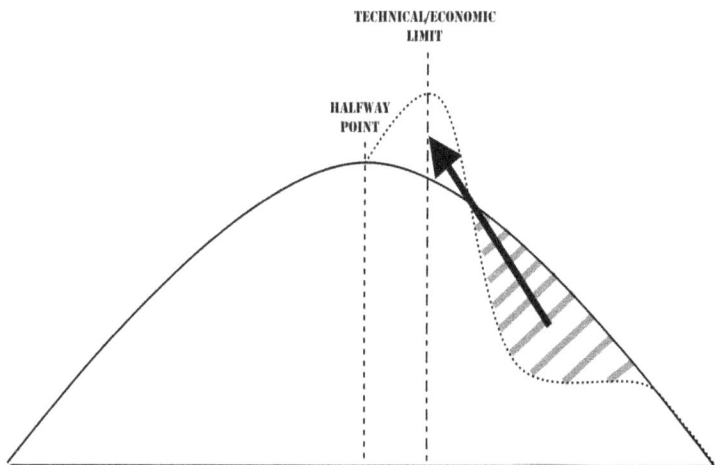

At present, this process is stunted because high energy prices serve to destroy economic demand. At its simplest, if more people are out of work, or have moved from full-time to part-time work, they need less fuel. Less obviously, the switch in consumer spending away from discretionary items serves to lower energy consumption across the economy. This, of course, appears to be where we are today. New oil recovery requires a price of $100 to be socially profitable (i.e. to provide the tax income, infrastructure maintenance, services, etc. necessary to the whole recovery process rather than just profits for investors) while prices above $50 destroy demand sufficiently to cause a recession.

In this sense, the date at which half of the global oil reserve has been consumed – which Hubbert thought would be around 2004 – is irrelevant because this does not include EROI in the equation. Global oil production has slowed significantly since 2000, while capital expenditure has increased dramatically[14] – exactly what would be anticipated as EROI declines. Techniques (fracking and tar sands) and locations (the Arctic and ultra-deep water) that would have been considered far too costly to invest in prior to 2005 have been developed in order to push production up to 97 million barrels a day. But this is merely technology fighting geology and EROI to a temporary standstill.

The downslope is less likely to involve queues of motorists outside empty filling stations, and more likely to involve millions of people giving up their cars.

[14] See e.g. Tverberg, G. 2014. *Beginning of the End? Oil Companies Cut Back on Spending.* https://ourfiniteworld.com/2014/02/25/beginning-of-the-end-oil-companies-cut-back-on-spending/ Tverberg shows that between 1884 and 1999, the compound annual growth rate of capital expenditure per barrel of oil was 0.9% whereas from 2000 to 2014 it rose 10.9%.

In 2007 the International Energy Agency smuggled this chart into its *World Energy Outlook*:

Oil production required to maintain global economic growth

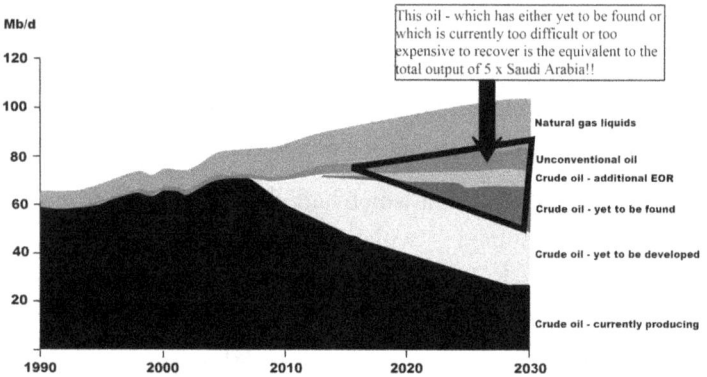

The chart was intended to reassure readers that the world would continue to enjoy growing volumes of oil up to at least 2030. But the chart included an area – which I have highlighted – that consists of resources that either have not been discovered or that are too expensive to recover. Taken together, these amount to more than five times the current production of Saudi Arabia. As a corrective to this optimism, we might note that the Ghawar oil field in Saudi Arabia, which was discovered in the 1930s, remains the largest oil deposit we have ever found. Moreover, we might note that we are currently burning our way through more than 10 times more oil than is being discovered. We might also note that much of what remains – like US shale deposits and Canadian tar sands – is expensive to produce, and that much of that industry is facing bankruptcy. Finally, we might observe that while natural gas liquids can be blended with oil, they are not a substitute for it.

High prices between 2010 and 2014 may have brought some of these resources into production. But massive disinvestment from the industry since mid-2014 is likely to have locked most of what remains away permanently.

A final problem facing the global economy is that demand for energy has increased remorselessly. China now consumes half of the entire global supply of coal. It also consumes half as much oil as The USA. And China's demand is rapacious. Other developing economies are also desperate for oil, including the oil-producing states themselves. Russia has claimed that it will cease exporting oil from 2018. Saudi Arabia has indicated that it will not be exporting oil beyond 2028.[15] This is not because these countries have run out of oil, but because their domestic economies have become ever more oil-dependent.

This problem is compounded by the growth of bilateral deals that remove oil from the global market. This leaves importing regions like Europe and the USA chasing a shrinking supply of oil to run what have become highly oil-dependent economies. This, in turn, is likely to produce price spikes that further crush demand and exacerbate economic decline.

[15] One reason why Saudi Arabia and Norway are pushing ahead with large-scale renewable energy deployment is to switch oil away from domestic consumption in order to maintain income-generating oil exports.

The problem with this for the developed economies is that oil (and fossil carbon in general) has a much higher marginal utility for people in developing countries. That is, whereas a spike in oil prices in the UK or the US would cause people to stop using oil for apparently frivolous activities, it would not prevent, for example, a Brazilian farmer from fuelling a tractor or an African smallholder from running a moped – the loss of value to them would be far greater.

In practice, then, energy supply constraints place a far greater relative burden upon developed economies than they do upon the developing world. However, these will not manifest in the form of fuel shortages. On the contrary, as the EROI cost of recovering and consuming oil increases, we are more likely to witness oil gluts because too few consumers in the developed economies can afford to consume at a price needed to keep energy companies profitable.

THE "ENERGY DEATH SPIRAL"

In the UK since 2010 the managers of National Grid – the company responsible for maintaining Britain's electricity and gas infrastructure – has been warning of the dangers of narrowing margins between supply and demand. In part this is because much of the energy infrastructure has reached the end of its life. Indeed, several nuclear power stations have been allowed to continue operating beyond their predicted closure date in order to maintain baseload supply. In part, the problem comes from the switch from coal to renewables to meet Britain's climate change commitments. Knowing that all of Britain's coal power stations must close by 2025, several operators have chosen to allow the ageing plants to close early rather than to continue to maintain them.

The latest UK government energy statistics show that between May and July 2016, coal accounted for just 5.3 percent of the country's energy. However, over the same period, energy from renewable sources fell by 23 percent; largely the result of unusually low wind speeds. With nuclear stable at 17.5 percent, it fell to largely imported gas to fill the gaps; providing more than half of the UK's energy during the quarter.

On three occasions since 2010, National Grid has been forced to deploy an emergency scheme in which heavy industrial energy users are disconnected in order to maintain household supply. The industries involved are then compensated for the losses they incur. Worryingly, the period since 2010 has seen a run of warm winters. So there is considerable concern that as capacity continues to fall until at least 2020, colder winters may see more widespread power outages – including the possibility of cuts to household energy.

Beyond capacity, however, is the problem of cost; itself a manifestation of falling EROI. This is impacting Britain from two directions. First, successive governments since the 1980s have ignored capacity and focused solely on holding prices down. Governments simply assumed that a free market in energy would deliver the infrastructure required to keep the lights on. As a result, much of the power generation capacity that should have replaced the ageing coal and nuclear power stations never got built. Although some renewables have been built in recent years, these barely scratch the surface of what is needed. At the same time, larger projects – such as the Hinkley Point C nuclear power plant – are unlikely to be completed in the time needed.

Second, the North Sea oil and gas supplies that governments blithely assumed would be available for decades to come have in fact crashed. Both oil and gas peaked in 1999, and production today is just a third of what was produced back then. Worse still, the current oil glut and low prices have caused a collapse in the North Sea industry, with a third of the jobs having been shed, and several large companies cancelling future extraction and bringing forward the decommissioning of existing fields. This means that the UK is increasingly dependent upon imported gas to keep the lights on. As competition heats up, the cost of this imported gas is likely to rise remorselessly.

One proposed solution to this predicament has been to encourage hydraulic fracturing on a similar scale to that in the USA. However, at present, nobody knows if there is *any* recoverable gas in the UK's shale deposits; still less whether gas can be extracted at a cost that will make it profitable. Again, EROI is the limiting factor. Unless UK gas can be profitably produced at a lower price than it can be imported for, then there is no benefit (and a lot of environmental drawbacks) to producing it.

As the EROI for fossil fuels has risen, renewable energy generation – especially rooftop photovoltaic solar – has become far more competitive; particularly when deployed at household level. Until recently, the UK government had been providing grants to households to install home solar systems, which also attract generous feed-in tariffs, through which energy companies purchase surplus solar energy from households. Even with the removal of government grants, there is still an advantage to those households who can still afford solar systems, not only through feed-in tariffs but also from the savings on running domestic appliances.

The cost of feed-in tariffs, together with any new generation capacity brought online is added onto customer bills rather than being paid out of general taxation. The result is that the cost of energy falls disproportionately on the poorest consumers.

Taken together, these conditions have created the potential for what several energy company CEOs have called the "energy death spiral".

Faced with increasing energy prices (due ultimately to falling EROI) consumers at either end of the income scale have an incentive to go "off grid". Affluent households will take advantage of the increasingly competitive solar systems to generate their own electricity. Poor households will shiver in the dark. In this way, both will try to avoid paying for energy; and as their numbers grow there will be huge political pressure to abandon the standing charges that are meant to cover the maintenance of the infrastructure. So the full cost of operating the Grid will fall onto a squeezed middle; those who can still afford to pay but who lack the capital to invest in getting off grid. Over time, those at either end of the squeezed middle will also go off grid as the rising cost of energy drives them away. Taken to its illogical conclusion, we would end up with a single household having to meet the entire cost of the grid. In reality, long before we reached that point, the grid would have become unprofitable and impossible to maintain.[16]

There are political work-arounds for this. Nationalisation or not-for-profit operation can stave off the day when the system collapses. The government could subsidise energy out of general taxation – although this would be just another way of removing money from businesses and households. But without raising EROI, these types of policy only kick the problem down the road.

Some forms of renewable energy help, some do not. For example, hydroelectric power makes absolute sense in Scandinavia but solar costs more to deploy than it provides in return. Geothermal is likely to make Iceland one of the most energy rich nations on Earth, but at such a northern latitude, solar makes little sense. Offshore wind and tidal

[16] Energy conservation measures, while curbing our impact on the environment, serve to exacerbate this problem.

generation makes sense for Atlantic-facing countries like Ireland, Scotland and Wales.[17] But the relationship between Germany and China is the exact opposite of what it should be – China (where there is far more sunlight) makes solar panels that are deployed in Germany (where there is not enough sunlight). Solar panels in Spain and Arizona can generate more than enough electricity for their regional needs; but solar deployed in New England, the UK or Northern Europe leaves these regions dependent upon imports.

In a global economy that is experiencing falling EROI, the problem is compounded by a lack of spare energy and capital to deploy in constructing a new energy infrastructure. Unlike currency, energy cannot be borrowed from the future. So the fact that a wind turbine will pay its energy investment back in five years' time is irrelevant if there is insufficient energy and capital today to allow it to be built and deployed. This problem becomes apparent when we look at energy density. The 31 square mile *Gwynt-y-Mor* offshore wind farm in North Wales – the second largest in the world – can produce 350 MW… in optimum conditions. The proposed tidal turbine farm off Shetland promises to deliver a similar 350 MW. Both cost billions of pounds to deploy. But taken together they produce less than half of the power generated by the coal-fired power station at Aberthaw in south Wales (which may close as early as 2017 – well ahead of schedule). Once we have to rely almost entirely on renewables, this

[17] Given the huge tidal range in the Severn Estuary – the second largest in the world – in EROI terms, a series of tidal lagoons should have been built in Wales before a single wind turbine was erected.

poses the thorny question of where we are going to find the energy for the replacement of the turbines when they wear out.

Remember that our twin needs are not just to replace the energy we currently derive from fossil carbon, but to *add* sufficient capacity to allow economic growth to continue. This, in turn, can only happen if we can find a means of squeezing up the EROI of renewables. As a back-of-an-envelope idea of what this might involve, consider the giant PS10 solar concentrator power station in the ideal conditions of the Spanish desert.[18]

"We know in theory, for example that a 254km2 array of solar panels in the Sahara Desert could replace all of the fossil fuels used to generate the electricity used in the global economy. However, solar panels cost energy, resources, capital and labour power – expressed in the global economy as time and money. If we consider the feat of engineering that is the giant PS10 solar generation plant near Seville in Spain, which covers just 1/423rd the area required to replace fossil fuels, we see why theory cannot be put into practice. PS10 cost 35 million euros, and took 4 years to build. Even a simple multiplication of this would mean that to replace fossil fuels with solar generation would cost 14.8 billion euros and would take 1,692 years to complete! There are, of course many other factors to take into account. More people could be put to work on the project to bring the

[18] Watkins, T. 2015. *The Consciousness of Sheep*. Waye Forward. P131.

time down. Economies of scale might bring the costs down. But beyond this, the essential truth is that the labour, energy and raw materials put into creating a solar replacement for fossil fuels are labour, energy and raw materials that must be taken from somewhere else in the global economy. Moreover, if exponential economic growth is to continue, any additional solar capacity that we do bring on stream is likely to be needed as an *additional* energy source rather than a *replacement*."

For the best part of three centuries, humanity has been able to borrow money from the future because we have had more than enough spare energy capacity to pay back the energy cost of the loan. As Professor Hall has observed, when you have that much spare energy, you can come up with pretty much any economic theory you like, and someone else will figure out a way of getting the economy growing again. Using solely the energy technologies available to us today, we are fast reaching a point at which we find ourselves in a zero sum game. The energy and capital we need to construct the next round of energy capacity can no longer come from a spare external reserve. Instead, it will have to be diverted from elsewhere in the economy.

When we reach that point, it will matter not one iota that this or that country has a derivative wealth of trillions of Dollars, Euros, Pounds, Yen or Yuan. Countries – like today's banks – will be wealthy only to the extent that on paper someone owes them those huge volumes of currency. Without the spare energy and capital to grow, in reality all of that paper is merely a claim on a future that will never arrive. This is because the same energy death spiral that will eventually kill the energy infrastructure will also kill the wider economy. As the amount of spare energy and capital shrinks, its cost must increase. We are witnessing this phenomenon playing out in the fossil fuel, mining and agricultural sectors today. Most of the global population are obliged to act like poor energy consumers; simply shivering in the dark because they can no longer meet the price required for industry to be profitable.

In practice this plays out almost imperceptibly. Collectively, we each take one less meal out, one less trip to the cinema, one less drive to the beach. We each choose to hold onto our old cars, televisions and phones just a few months longer. Across the economy, businesses that have to grow in order to service their debts experience these individual choices as a fall in demand. So they too begin to scale back on their spending and future investment, while lowering the price of goods they have already produced. This results in a generalised deflation which begins to feed upon itself as people put off spending in anticipation of falling prices. At the same time, unemployment and under employment increase and workers' wages fall, causing demand across the economy to fall further. This destroys the economic "Goldilocks zone" where we can arrive at a price at which consumers can afford to buy and firms can afford to produce. Supply and demand itself breaks down – most likely in the form of price volatility.

This, however, is merely the surface ripple of a much more profound problem. Our economy has been built on cheap and easily accessible energy. Over three centuries this allowed us to take advantage of huge economies of scale through what economists and management theorists call "efficiency measures." A farm, for example, is much more efficient if it specialises in the production of a single cash crop than if it tries to produce a range of different crops. Similarly, it is far more efficient for several car or aeroplane manufacturers to make use of the same engines than it would be if each constructed their own. It makes absolutely no sense for individual companies – still less households – to install their own energy grids, transportation systems, water supplies, communications networks or sewage treatment systems. Every country benefits from the efficiency of having just one each of these critical infrastructures.

Physicist David Korowicz poses an interesting thought experiment: Imagine what would happen if all of the computer processing chips that were made in the last five years stopped working for some reason.

Korowicz's point is that we would not simply go back to the situation that existed in 2011. Our entire critical infrastructure today depends upon advanced computer control. Were the computers themselves to fail, *everything* would stop working. Water would not flow and sewage could not be treated. We would have no electricity, gas or fuel for our vehicles. Public transport would fail. Food storage facilities would go offline, leaving meagre food supplies to rot. Shops would be unable to take electronic payments, while banks would be unable to dispense cash. If we were unable to bring the computers quickly back online, our entire way of life would collapse.

How is it possible that the failure of components that have only been in place for five years would totally undermine our way of life when we were fine five years ago? The answer is that as we have increased the complexity of our economy, we need to harness and focus an increasing volume of energy to keep the system going. Take out the computer chips and we are no longer able to control and focus the energy. Without the energy, the system collapses.

Fortunately, the computer chips are not about to fail. However, thinking about how our globalised critical infrastructure is integrated allows us to see its vulnerability. In essence, efficiency is the enemy of resilience. The benefits we enjoy from efficiency – in terms of cheaper prices in the developed countries – are only achieved at the cost of increasing vulnerability to both external and internal shocks.

Korowicz argues that a banking and financial collapse similar to the one that began in 2008, could have a similar impact to a collapse of the transport system. Without insurances and letters of credit, trust in the system would break down. At the time of writing, the seventh biggest shipping line on Earth – Hanjin shipping – has collapsed, with the result that ships have been stuck outside ports around the world because ports refuse to let them dock for fear that they will not get paid. In a global banking collapse, this type of problem would afflict the entire global transportation system and much else besides.

Like bank crashes, the energy death spiral is just another way in which the critical infrastructure on which we depend for our way of life will come tumbling down. In September 2000, five days of fuel protests brought Britain close to a collapse. Behind the scenes, the UK government had introduced emergency measures to maintain its own command and control systems and to alleviate some of the worst impacts on the nation's food supplies, health services and transport system. The protest were called off a day or two before these measures would have come into force. However, evidence of a breakdown was already apparent. Shops were out of food, filling stations were out of fuel and public transport was forced to limit services. Hospitals struggled in the face of falling supplies.[19] Remarkably, it later transpired that 90 percent of the commercial deliveries in the UK had actually got through more or less as normal. It turned out that a loss of just 10 percent of capacity was sufficient to drive an entire country into a state of emergency.

Korowicz's warning of a cascading collapse, in which a collapse in any one critical infrastructure impacts on all of the others, may be too dramatic. Falling EROI is not going to impact on the entire energy infrastructure all at once. Rather, we are more likely to live through a period of intermittency in which the process of going about our daily lives becomes more difficult and more expensive. For example, when we reach the point at which supply shortages spill across the business sector and from industry to households, things that we take for granted become more

[19] This was a manifestation of Liebig's law of the minimum, which holds that systems fail as a result of a shortage in the least available input rather than shortages across the board. In UK hospitals in September 2000, operations were cancelled because of a shortage of stiches.

difficult. Withdrawing cash or shopping becomes less predictable if power supplies randomly fail. Running businesses – particularly those that depend upon computers – gets more difficult; not least because power failures damage computer hardware. Costs – and prices – increase as households and companies seek work-arounds (such as deploying their own back-up generation).

The problem is that the work-arounds that we deploy in a falling EROI environment either individually (e.g. home/business renewable energy systems) or collectively (e.g. state energy subsidies) serve merely to divert energy and capital from elsewhere in the economy. The price of keeping the lights on comes at the cost of business failures and economic decay elsewhere.

The options facing humanity are stark. If EROI continues to fall, we will be left with insufficient energy to maintain the complexity we have built into the modern global economy. This will impact particularly badly on the developed nations, where the marginal benefits of expensive energy are lower. That is, from a low level of energy use, developing and under-developed parts of the planet are better placed to adapt. Developed countries, by contrast are likely to see whole systems break down. The *only* way out is to find a means of increasing EROI once more. And at present, no such means exist.

IMAGINED FUTURES

For Marx, the key to the future lay in workers realising both the degree of their exploitation and the power that this gave them. The general strike would bring the exploiters to their knees. The popular revolution would sweep away the old political order. Gradually, as the science and technology built by capitalism was deployed for the common good, the need for a political state would wither away; replaced by an age of plenty.

Workers still enjoy the power to bring the old order to its knees. For although labour is not the source of value; it is largely the means by which value (energy) is deployed. This said, the established order has succeeded in marginalising and disempowering working people. Breaking trade unions, offshoring jobs and extending credit have all been deployed to crush organised resistance. Even in the most democratic states, special measures and emergency powers have been put in place against the day when ordinary people take to the streets in protest at the old order.

The darkly amusing part of all of this is that while the ruling elites have taken Marx's Labour Theory of Value and its potential consequences very seriously, working people for the most part have not. Indeed, as the economic order has disintegrated in the aftermath of the 2008 crash, people have looked to proto-fascist populists for their salvation. Laughably, it is these false populists who promise to restore the very capitalism of the free market that Marx assumed people would want to overthrow. Meanwhile, it is the ruling elite that has systematically overthrown both market capitalism and democracy; replacing it with a deformed caricature of the Stalinist system that prevailed in Eastern Europe between 1945 and 1989.

All the while, of course, the real proletariat upon which the wealth and privilege was built – the millions of unseen, uncomplaining fossil carbon energy slaves – were beginning a revolt of their own. From the very start of the Industrial Revolution the energy slaves had been burping and farting out obnoxious gases into the atmosphere. But as the economy expanded and globalised after 1945, these greenhouse gases began to change the climate in a way that began to threaten the very habitat that allows human life on the planet.

During the expansion of the economy in the twentieth century, GDP doubled four times. But in order to achieve that growth energy consumption doubled *eighty* times! And from the 1970s, the energy slaves achieved something that mere working people could never manage – they successfully forced the ruling elite to give them an irrevocable pay rise. From the 1970s the cost of obtaining energy began to increase in a way that impacted upon the economy. This obliged the elites in the developed countries to make three work-arounds:

○ Dilute the cost of labour at home by bringing women into the workforce

○ Offshore jobs to parts of the world that still had cheap labour and poor working conditions

○ Extend credit to the majority of the population in order to maintain consumption-based growth.

Had the problem confronting them been a rise in the cost of labour alone, they might have got away with it. But the increased pressure on wages in the 1970s was merely an expression of the impact of higher energy costs throughout the economy. Workers needed more money to fund higher energy costs just at the point where businesses were themselves struggling to meet their own energy constraints.

In 1943, management theorist Leslie White had devised what is now known as White's Law:

> "Culture evolves as the amount of energy harnessed per capita per year is increased or as the efficiency of the instrumental means of putting the energy to work is increased".

From the mid-1970s in the developed countries, the amount of energy per capita began to decline. Against this, however, the 1970s also witnessed a series of technological improvements to energy efficiency – most obviously seen in the revolution in computing in the 1980s. But these technological efficiency measures suffer from diminishing returns. The big energy savings of the 1980s and 1990s gave way to increasingly expensive energy "shavings" in the early 2000s. And by the 2010s, corporations had resorted to cheating on efficiency tests rather than making real improvements because the cost of the fines if they get caught is less than the costs involved in making further energy efficiencies. In the end, no matter how skilled the engineers and technologists, the laws of thermodynamics set hard physical limits on energy – we cannot get more or even the equivalent out than we put in.

In the fossil carbon space, we have now passed the EROI point at which advanced societies are possible. That we still have access to massive deposits of oil and gas shale, tar sands and ultra-deep water oil is not the point. If we cannot get these resources out of the ground at an EROI greater than 20:1, then with each month that goes by the societies that they are meant to operate will decline even further. We can distort this problem for a while by using debt to (in effect) steal other countries' energy to pay for our shortfall by increasing our national current account debt. However, once investors in those other countries wake up to the fact that we are never going to pay them back, the ability to do this will go away forever.

Renewables do not particularly help here either. At a local level, rooftop solar, tilted to gather maximum sunlight (in the UK this means on a south-facing rooftop) can provide an EROI of 20:1. Similarly, an offshore wind turbine facing out toward the Atlantic Ocean can provide 20:1. However, this is only in optimal conditions and for that single deployment. But to replace fossil carbon, renewables have to cover vast areas in order to concentrate enough energy to make a difference. For this reason, what counts is not the EROI on a single turbine or solar array, but the EROI of all of the turbines and arrays deployed.[20] If, for example, someone were foolish enough to deploy solar panels on a flat surface, where they are often shaded, and where they are susceptible to damage and erosion – for example a solar

[20] With fossil carbon fuels this issue doesn't arise because the chemistry of oil, gas and coal means that they have a fairly standard energy density after they have been refined.

roadway like the ones the French government wants to build – this is not just a waste of energy and money in and of itself, but serves also to lower the EROI of all solar systems. In the same way, deploying wind turbines on the leeward side of buildings – as practiced by the Welsh government – serves to lower the EROI of wind as a whole.

So long as we have enjoyed the luxury of cheap fossil carbon fuels, this kind of EROI wastage has only been a problem in climate change terms – each badly deployed renewable generator is merely an unnecessary additional dose of greenhouse gases into an already dangerously polluted atmosphere. However, as the cheap fossil carbon goes away, EROI becomes a matter of life and death because energy used to deploy badly situated technology is energy that was taken away from the optimal deployment of technology elsewhere.

This has yet to become a public discussion largely because we continue to think of value in Marxist terms, and this allows us to pretend that money is entirely abstracted from the physical world. We simply assume that governments and firms can print or borrow currency to deploy as many new renewable energy arrays as they want. But money is only really a claim on the use of energy. And as spare energy capacity goes away, we will discover that bringing new currency into existence merely lowers the value of the currency rather than mobilising energy and resources in the way we intended.

It is possible that a more authoritarian government would be able to act to prevent the misuse of the remaining energy –

although authoritarian governments have generally been the worst at understanding science, and the most profligate at diverting energy and resources to their favoured followers rather than deploying them for the public good. Democracy is unlikely to prove any better. It is worth considering, for example, that the current UK government is looking to invest a decade of scarce energy and resources on such white elephant projects as the expansion of Heathrow, widespread hydraulic fracturing and an associated gas infrastructure, HS2, and Hinkley Point C; all of which are likely to be completely worthless by the time they are complete.

An economy based on renewable energy cannot avoid being radically different to the modern global economy. There are huge gains to be made from energy conservation measures, but these are impossible within an economic system that depends upon growth for its existence. Nevertheless these measures have to be made if we are to optimise renewable energy technologies. By necessity this economy will have to be more localised if we are to preserve those parts of our transport system (such as the production and movement of food) that will continue to require oil. Again, this means taking measures that are at odds with the growth paradigm. And there is, of course, the inherent risk that even if these measures are taken, our societal EROI will still be too low to support the most energy dependent specialisations found within the global economy.

Some of these specialisations have already gone. Space travel all but ended in 1972. Today, the USA does not even have the technology and skills to transport astronauts into the low orbit of the International Space Station. For all the talk of colonising Mars (a six month journey), we currently lack the capacity even to send people back to the Moon (a three day journey). Similarly, supersonic flight came to an end in November 2003 when the Concordes were retired. Occasionally an Elon Musk or a Richard Branson will pop up to revive the idea, but once the government grants run out, it becomes obvious that there is no way of getting a return on the investment and the project is quietly dropped.

We might have already scaled the heights of medicine and engineering. As the EROI scales back and the money runs out, we may soon lose advanced treatments for cancer, research into nuclear fusion, and a host of other ultra-high-tech human activities that have insufficient impact on the daily lives of most people. Exactly what we get to keep and what we get to lose will be determined by the choices we have been making since the 1970s when we were first warned about the likely consequences of trying to achieve infinite growth on a finite planet. As American essayist John Michael Greer warns:[21]

"Once easily accessible fossil fuels started to become scarce, and more and more energy and other resources had to be invested in the extraction of what remained, problems started to crop up. Tar sands and oil shales in their natural form are not as concentrated an energy source as light sweet crude—once they're refined, sure, the differences are minimal, but a whole system analysis of energy concentration has to start at the moment each energy source enters the system. Take a cubic yard of

[21] Greer, J.M. 2015. *As Night Closes In.*
http://www.resilience.org/stories/2015-02-05/as-night-closes-in

tar sand fresh from the pit mine, with the sand still in it, or a cubic yard of oil shale with the oil still trapped in the rock, and you've simply got less energy per unit volume than you do if you've got a cubic yard of light sweet crude fresh from the well, or even a cubic yard of good permeable sandstone with light sweet crude oozing out of every pore.

"It's an article of faith in contemporary culture that such differences don't matter, but that's just another aspect of our cornucopian myth. The energy needed to get the sand out of the tar sands or the oil out of the shale oil has to come from somewhere, and that energy, in turn, is not available for other uses. The result, however you slice it conceptually, is that the upper limit of complexity begins moving down. That sounds abstract, but it adds up to a great deal of very concrete misery, because as already noted, the complexity of a society determines such things as the number of different occupational specialties it can support, the number of employees who are involved in the production and distribution of a given good or service, and so on. There's a useful phrase for a sustained contraction in the usual measures of complexity in a human ecosystem: "economic depression."…

"Adding to our total stock of knowledge won't change that result, since knowledge is a necessary condition for economic expansion but not a sufficient one: if the upper limit of complexity set by the laws of thermodynamics drops below the level that your knowledge base would otherwise support, further additions to the knowledge base simply mean that there will be a growing number of things that people know how to do in theory, but that nobody has the resources to do in practice."

In this future, humankind is stuck in a slow motion collapse in which the things that we take for granted today gradually break down. Eventually a combination of energy conservation and renewable energy deployment will stabilise our localised economies at a much lower level of complexity. Of necessity, this will involve a significant collapse in the human population to that which can be supported with minimal industrial agriculture. This need not involve anything apocalyptic, but can be achieved by the scaling back of life expectancy similar to that seen following the collapse of the Soviet Union. A small percentage increase in stillbirths and childhood deaths, coupled to a decade less life expectancy, and we are back to 3 billion people in a couple of generations.

Anyone who is not a tree-hugging hippy is unlikely to find this renewables vision of our energy future particularly appealing. But without stepping outside the laws of physics, it is hard to see how we avoid that kind of future. This said, the laws of physics do offer a way out – albeit one that many will find equally unpalatable.

When Frederick Soddy was considering the causes of the 1929 crash and the ensuing depression, he observed that:

"If atomic energy is ever tapped, an outburst of human activity would occur such as would make the triumphs of our times seem tawdry, and primitive humanity's struggle for energy as the fantastic memory of some horrid dream."

When we consider energy density, in comparison with renewable energy generation fossil fuels are off the scale. Wind, tidal and solar energy are so diffuse that they do not register at all – at 10.3 mega joules per kilogram (MJ/Kg), a ham and cheese sandwich has a greater energy density. Diesel oil has an energy density of 48 MJ/Kg. The uranium fuel in a thorium breeder reactor has an energy density of 79,420,000 MJ/Kg. This is a measure of the difference between chemical and nuclear energy.

Now the obvious objection here is that nuclear energy is dangerous and polluting. Accidents like the ones at Chernobyl in 1986 and Fukushima in 2011 demonstrate that nuclear power stations are a major safety hazard. And even without accidents, the waste created will be dangerously radioactive for thousands of years. Nuclear power might also be little more than a dangerous means of kicking the can down the road; because although there is still a few decades worth of uranium available to us, this is only because most of our energy comes from fossil fuels. If we switched over to nuclear, we would soon exhaust the world's accessible uranium deposits. After which we would be back to declining EROI but we will have added a nuclear waste problem to our other difficulties (spent nuclear fuel rods have to be artificially cooled for around a decade before they can be moved to storage).

There are several myths in these objections. First is the idea that nuclear fission is what makes nuclear power dangerous.

At both Fukushima and Chernobyl (and the near miss at Three Mile Island) the danger came not from the reaction but from the means by which heat was converted into electricity. These reactors were effectively bolted onto the same turbine system used in a coal or gas power station. Thus, the reactors had to transfer heat from the reactor into water. But as every schoolboy knows, water boils at 100 degrees centigrade at sea level. To get sufficient heat to drive the turbines, the water has to be pressurised. Most of the nuclear power stations in use today use pressure to heat water to more than 350 degrees. To do this, they require a special pressure vessel cast as a single piece of metal. Only one steelworks on earth – in Japan – is able to do this.

This configuration is fine(ish) so long as nothing goes wrong. But when things go wrong, to prevent an explosion in the pressure vessel, steam has to be vented into the larger containment hall. When this is done, the steam tends to break down into hydrogen and oxygen gas. If anything causes a spark, the result – as at Chernobyl and Fukushima – is that the containment hall explodes; often spraying a lot of radioactive material into the atmosphere.

So there is a very good safety argument against the further use of pressurised water reactors. But not all nuclear reactors depend upon water as a medium to transfer heat.

The second myth is that all nuclear waste is *waste*. Spent fuel is waste because it cannot be used (in old nuclear reactors). However, some of the "waste" plutonium 238 is essential for powering the satellites that we send to the outer solar system (beyond the range where solar panels no longer work). As things stand, NASA is unable to send any more missions beyond Mars because there is insufficient plutonium 238. Xenon gas is used across industries. Some short-lived (and thus extremely radioactive) fission products have important medical uses. Other products are useful to industry.

Much of the waste that is produced is a result of the type of reactor used rather than being an inevitable problem with nuclear power. A pressurised water reactor will burn just 0.5 percent of the uranium fuel. The remainder has to be stored as waste. The reason we inherited these highly inefficient pressurised water reactors owes more to various governments' desire to obtain nuclear weapons than to any serious consideration of the best methods for generating energy.

Today, there are several so-called fourth-generation nuclear power systems that are not only capable of using far more of the fuel, but can even use much of the waste that we are currently struggling to find safe storage for. Crucially, two of the latest fourth-generation reactors do not use water to transfer heat. Liquid metal and liquid molten salt reactors use materials with a much higher melting point than the 350 degrees of pressurised water. These reactors cannot cause Chernobyl and Fukushima-type disasters because the greater heat allows them to operate at normal pressure. More importantly, they can be configured for passive safety. That is, in the event of a control failure the fuel is passively removed from the reactor, so that fission stops. Even if a terrorist put a gun to the head of an operative and ordered him/her to cause a meltdown, it would be impossible to do.

In at least one of the proposed designs, water is removed from the process altogether. Instead, super-heated carbon dioxide is used to transfer the heat from the reactor to the turbines. The big advantage with this is that the giant turbine halls associated with coal, gas and pressurised water nuclear power stations are not needed. Instead, a turbine just a few metres long would be sufficient to match the 1GW output of a coal or gas power station.

Because of the energy density of the atomic nucleus, fourth-generation nuclear (and beyond) has the potential to produce more energy than we could currently think of uses for. With excess energy we could afford to suck carbon out of the atmosphere. We could even synthesise liquid fuels from air or sea water. We could easily desalinate water, allowing us to obviate one of the looming climate catastrophes. Indeed, we could generate enough clean water to convert deserts back to fertile land.

Unlike the mythical nuclear *fusion*, prototype liquid metal and molten salt reactors have already been built and operated. Reassuringly, the physicists who operated them said that they were boring (they were uneventful to operate)… which is exactly what you want to be told about nuclear power. These fourth generation reactors are beginning to be developed around the world. Indeed, China has obtained most of the American research papers into molten salt thorium reactors and is actively pursuing them as a means of weaning itself off its over-reliance on coal and oil. The UK government has also given the go-ahead for an experimental molten salt reactor in Britain.

For better or worse, the problem of energy density means that only nuclear power offers the possibility of a return to an abundant energy economy in future. For the most part, renewables take us to an energy-poor future in which we are obliged to operate at a far lower level of complexity than is possible today. Neither option is right or wrong. Each comes with benefits and problems of its own.

Each energy source that we have used throughout history was accompanied by a suite of technologies. Coal was accompanied by railways, factories, steamships and ports. Oil was accompanied by highways, airports, tractors, cars, vans and aeroplanes. Electricity brought telecommunications and computing. But each depended upon abundant high EROI energy for its maintenance. And each was built on top of the other.

We can only begin to guess at the types of technologies that we might unlock with a combination of renewables and new nuclear. All we can say is that such a future would be as baffling to us as our technology would be to the average resident of the late eighteenth century.

The choice is ours. On our present trajectory we risk the very worst of all worlds. We are rapidly losing the EROI we need even to maintain our current way of life. And as things break down, our ability to boost future EROI is decaying. Eventually we could lose almost all of our energy entirely, and find ourselves forced to cannibalise the achievements of today's civilisation. As Greer notes, a medieval blacksmith could go a long way with just one of the reinforced steel joists from a modern concrete building.

But if this happens, running oncology departments, driving cars or taking holidays abroad will be a distant memory.

Alternatively, we can start to take energy seriously. If we have the humility to understand that most of our achievements over the past three centuries were less the result of our ingenuity and more the product of abundant cheap energy, we may just begin to move toward the kind of eco-technic future offered by groups like the Zeitgeist Movement and the Venus Project.

What is certain is that no amount of offshoring, union-busting and oppressive policing on the part of the global elite is going to thwart the revolt of the energy slaves. From here on in, the cost of energy is going to increase even as the EROI ratio drops to zero. The rate of profit and the rate of productivity will fall relentlessly. Our standard of living – especially in the developed countries – is going to decline rapidly. Unchecked we will find that a growing proportion of the energy we generate will have to go into producing energy. At the same time, a growing proportion of the currency we create and obtain will have to be channelled into servicing the debts that we ran up back in the days when we thought fossil fuels would last forever. As both processes take hold, what we think of as our way of life will wither on the vine; starved of both energy and capital.

If we allow this to happen, then climate change – which is already baked in – is going to be no more than the final nail in the coffin of a civilisation long past its use-by date.

The choice is ours…

ALSO BY TIM WATKINS

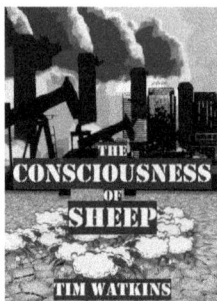

The Consciousness of Sheep provides a detailed and thoroughly researched explanation of the current predicament of Western civilisation; the ways in which the crises are likely to unfold; and the progressive responses that are beginning to emerge.

It is a fascinating read for anyone with an interest in economics, energy and the environment.

Austerity - will kill the economy! That is the stark message in this brief guide to the imminent failure of the policies adopted in Europe, the UK and the USA in the aftermath of the crisis of 2008.

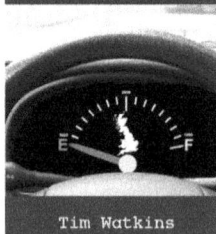

North Sea oil and gas production peaked in 1999. Britain's coal industry was destroyed in 1985. Its ageing fleet of nuclear power stations are coming to the end of their lives. The UK government is recklessly gambling on shale gas that simply may not exist.

At the same time, imported energy is getting harder to come by. And we have invested far too little in renewables. *Britain's coming energy crisis* explains why the lights may be about to go out… perhaps for good.

The Root of All Evil: The problem of debt-based money In this book, social scientist Tim Watkins walks us through the way the debt-based money system operates, and explains the dire consequences that await us if we refuse to change the way our money works.